GRAHAM DUNKLEY

AUSTRALIAN
fabian
SOCIETY

90 0385415 8

Australia: Strategies for Renewal is a series of pamphlets designed to promote constructive debate of the major social, economic and industrial issues confronting Australia.

The series is published by the Australian Fabian Society, Socialist Forum and Pluto Press (Australia). None of these organisations adopts policy positions of their own, and the pamphlets represent the views solely of their authors.

Series editor: John Mathews
Series editorial committee: Australian Fabian Society —
Ken Coghill, Gary Jungworth, Meg Paul;
Socialist Forum —
Julia Gillard, John Mathews, Mark Taft.

First published in 1992 by Pluto Press Australia Limited,
PO Box 199, Leichhardt, NSW 2040
in association with the Australian Fabian Society,
PO Box 2707X, Melbourne, Vic 3001 and
Socialist Forum, PO Box 1056, Carlton, Victoria 3053

Copyright © Graham Dunkley

Cover design: Trevor Hood

Typeset by Asset Typesetting Pty Ltd, Leichhardt, NSW 2040

Printed and bound on recycled paper by
Southwood Press, 80 Chapel Street, Marrickville, NSW 2204

Australian Cataloguing in Publication Data

Dunkley, Graham, 1946–.
The greening of the red: sustainability, socialism and the environmental crisis.

Bibliography.
ISBN 0 949138 80 0.

1. Environmental protection — Australia. 2. Economic development — Environmental aspects — Australia.
3. Environmental policy — Australia. 4. Socialism — Australia.
I. Australian Fabian Society. II. Socialism Forum.
III Title. (Series: Australia, strategies for renewal).

333.720994.

CONTENTS

• PREFACE

THIS book is about what I consider to be the great question of our age — that vast complex of problems usually called the 'environmental issue' which challenges so many of the assumptions upon which our industrial society and our ideological models, whether capitalist or socialist, are based. Coming at a time when socialism is facing the greatest challenge in its history, I argue that the environment crisis is a critical consideration in seeking new directions for socialism. The book is an outcome of many years teaching, political activity, environmental activism, reading, talking and frustrating efforts to establish an alternative rural sustainable community. I am indebted to many people for information and stimulating discussions on the issues, particularly Daryl Sipos, David Holmgren, David Cheadle, Tony Murphy, Phil Sutton and others from the Melbourne Environmental Economics Group. I am grateful to John Mathews, Clem Tisdell and Jay Menon for comments and guidance, but especially to Jenny Crawford for all the above assistance and more. Residual deficiencies are entirely my own. I wish to thank John Mathews for initiating the project, Gary Jungwirth for procedural assistance and the Fabian Society — Socialist Forum for sponsoring it. For the thankless task of typing I thank, in particular, Joyce Jones, Margaret Micallef and Angela Billing.

Terminology in this field is a problem at present because of the plethora of vaguely defined positions held. I will use the words *environmentalist* and *conservationist* for people in some way actively engaged in environmental and/or conservation advocacy. The word *Greens* (upper case) will refer to people formally involved in an environmental party or group and acting in that capacity. *Ecologists* are people engaged in the science of ecology, a sub-discipline of biology. For general streams of thought I have coined the following terms — *expansionists* (advocates of continuing maximum long-term growth), *precautionists* (those who see some problems and accept slower growth) and *conservators* (those who see major problems and may want to stop most growth or even reverse it). As adjectives, *environmental* and *green* refer to the broad range of problems now manifest, while *ecological* refers more specifically to the processes in nature as studied by ecologists. The terms 'blue', 'red', 'green' and other shades between are used only in the context of the environmental debate and are discussed extensively in Section 5. The word *socialist* refers broadly to the whole range of people and movements who at various times have opposed in any way the established capitalist system. Distinctions within the category are made where necessary.

I reluctantly use the US definition of billion (1,000 million) and trillion (1,000 billion) because of their common use, though I prefer the traditional terms milliard and billion as they are logical and more consistant with usage in other languages. All dollars are Australian unless otherwise specified.

• ABBREVIATIONS

AFR	—	*Australian Financial Review*
BCA	—	Business Council of Australia, the leading national umbrella body for Australian business organisations
CFCs	—	Chlorofluorocarbons
CPS	—	Centrally Planned Socialism (or Socialist)
EC	—	European Community
ECSSOS	—	Ecologically and Socially Sustainable Organisation of Systems, my substitute term for 'sustainable development'
EPA	—	Environmental Protection Authority (Agency in the US)
GATT	—	General Agreement on Tarrifs and Trade — the body which oversees international trading relations
GDP and GNP	—	Gross Domestic (National) Product, the most common measures of national income, GDP being exclusive of external income flows
GHGs	—	Greenhouse Gases
GW	—	*Guardian Weekly*
NEG	—	Negative Economic Growth
OECD	—	Organisation for Economic Co-operation and Development, a loose umbrella body for all Western industrial countries
RAC	—	Resources Assessment Commission, Australia
RETP	—	Resource and Energy Throughput, a term coined by Boulding and commonly used for the total of all resources and energy used in an economy per annum
SD	—	Sustainable Development
SOS	—	Sustainably Organised Systems, an abbreviation of ECSSOS
TNCs	—	Trans-national Companies (Corporations)
UN	—	United Nations
WCED	—	World Commission on Environment and Development
ZPG	—	Zero Population Growth

Box 1 Quotations Referred to in the Text

1. You are left ... with something rather like the skeleton of a body wasted by disease; the rich, soft soil has all run away leaving the land nothing but skin and bone.
    Plato on soil erosion in ancient Greece (*Critias*, Penguin, 1965:132).

2. If the earth must lose that great portion of its pleasantness which it owes to things that the unlimited increase of wealth and population would extirpate ... I sincerely hope, for the sake of posterity, that they will be content to be stationary, long before necessity compels them to it ... a stationary condition of capital and population implies no stationary state of human improvement.
    John Stuart Mill.[1]

3. Those machines of which the civilized world is so proud, has it any right to be proud of the use they have been put to by Commercial war and waste ...
    Think of the spreading sore of London swallowing up with its loathsomeness field and wood and heath without mercy and without hope ... (or of) the Black horror and reckless squalor of our manufacturing districts so dreadful to the senses which are unused to them that it is ominous for the future of the race ...
    William Morris.[2]

4. When the Press clamours that the one thing needed to make this island an Arcadia is productivity, and more productivity, and yet more productivity, that is Industrialism. It is confusion of means with ends ... So they destroy religion and art and morality, which cannot exist unless they are disinterested; and having destroyed these, which are the end, for the sake of industry, which is a means, they make their industry what they make their cities, a desert of unnatural dreariness.
    R. H. Tawney (1921:44–5).

5. The stuff of the upper half of the hourglass represents available matter-energy, which continuously pours

down into the lower half and, by this very fact, becomes unavailable matter-energy. To show that this degradation is irrevocable, we shall specify that *this* hourglass cannot be turned upside down.

> Nicholas Georgescu-Roegen (in Daly and Umana 1981:63).

6. Many of the development paths of the industrialised nations are clearly unsustainable.

> Dr. Gro Harlem Brundtland, Prime Minister of Norway and Chairwoman of the WCED (1990:xvi).

7. Sustainable global development requires that those who are more affluent adopt life-styles within the planet's ecological means ... (and that) population size and growth are in harmony with the changing productive potential of the ecosystem.

> The World Commission on Environment and Development (WCED, 1990:9).

1 INTRODUCTION

FOR those who have long believed in the Soviet system as an alternative to capitalism the unthinkable has happened. It now seems clear, particularly since the abortive coup of August 1991, that the Marxist-Leninist system is being disbanded, and that the Soviet Union itself is breaking up. To the old faithful, and even to disillusioned socialists who had hoped for a reformed Soviet-style model, an apparently eternal verity has been lost on the eve of its seventy-fifth anniversary. Few will mourn the loss of totalitarianism and the Stalinist horrors it spawned. Some may rue the collapse of the centrally planned socialist (CPS) economy which once seemed a viable model for the development. Many, however, rightly fear that the traditional socialist aspiration for an equitable society may be lost in an unplanned dash for growth and an obscene scramble by Western interests for morsels from the corpse of communism.

The widespread boast by the media and Western leaders that CPS systems have collapsed through neglect of the market and suppression of acquisitiveness is a simplistic, self-serving rationalisation. What has collapsed is just one model of socialism from among several aspirants, and it has waned more because of totalitarian oppression, bureaucratism, excessive centralism, materialism, environmental neglect, corruption and denial of spiritual values than because of the infeasibility of socialism *per se*. The CPS systems have collapsed partly because they were unable to challenge capitalism on its home ground — the satisfaction of materialistic wants. Certainly central planning is cumbersome and unsuited to affluence. Ultimately, however, the CPS models collapsed as much for political and cultural reasons as through economic factors. In spurning democracy and scorning spirituality they generated the sorts of materialist demands which capitalism is better able to satisfy. Today former CPS countries have a unique and exciting opportunity to develop new democratic socialist models if they can manage to elude the massive Western pressures towards full blown capitalism.

In the West even traditional social democratic and welfarist models seem to be in retreat as New Right doctrines take root amongst decision-makers and Labour governments take up positions formerly held by Liberal parties. However, I argue that this has been a victory for politics rather than for correctness. Whilst the New Right may be correct about matters such as over-regulation and bureaucratism, it is wrong in many critical respects, some of which will be noted in this book.

For the moment capitalism appears to have won a remarkable victory, as its genius lies in its ability to both create and satisfy material wants. No other model of human society can challenge capitalism in this arena. I argue, however, that this will prove a short-lived Pyrrhic victory in a crumbling colesseum, both because Western industrial capitalism still retains some residual economic instabilities and because it faces worsening socio-cultural and environmental crises. Some of these crises, such as urban congestion, decaying infrastructure and cyclical unemploy-ment are self-inflicted through the adoption of New Right policies, so are potentially curable under the existing system. Other crises, such as poverty, alienation, drug-taking, global cultural homogenisation and the decay of traditions are substantially due to inappropriate technologies and social structures, so may eventually be curable with modifications to the existing system, though I am sceptical. But many social inequities and environmental problems are due fundamentally to the socially and ecologically unsustainable nature of industrial capitalism, and so cannot be cured without drastic change.

Capitalism has proved very good at achieving badly-conceived goals.

This book is about environmental issues, but in the wider context of the problems of industrial capitalism and the potential for socialist solutions. When green activists first raised environmental concerns, many of the Left were sceptical about the issues and hostile to proposed anti-industrial responses, often asserting that any such problems lay in capitalism not industrialism. Today most of the Left accepts environmental concerns, even if opportunistically so on the part of some, but many still believe in democratic socialist industrial solutions. It is therefore not generally true, as many of the Right hold, that anti-capitalist forces have merely changed their colours from red to green — from 'reds under beds' to 'greens behind screens'. New concerns and philosophies are involved. The world has changed and new imperatives are arising.

I argue in this book that today's problems lie with both capitalism and industrialism, so that both must change. Industrialism differs from pre-industrial society by its intensive use of capital, resources, energy, technology, information and chemicals, by its urban globalism, by its extreme pressure on ecosystems, by its syntheticness and by its repudiation of spiritual cultures and traditions. I will often refer to this as the 'machine-chemical' model, whether capitalist or socialist in form. I argue that this model will not be socially or ecologically sustainable for much longer due to the costs of, and limits to, the growth mechanisms upon which it relies. This model, in all its Western capitalist, CPS and Third World manifestations, has brought us to the frontiers of the Earth's capacity to provide resources and absorb wastes. Not only must policies change, but entire systems must alter. Western cynics have said that turning around a CPS economy is like turning an ocean liner, but I suggest that turning around a greed-based, materialist economy is like turning an entire harbour.

I also argue that the current fashion of seeking to reconcile environment and economics through new models of 'sustainable development' (SD) are flawed, that oft proffered panaceas, such as markets and technology, are over-rated and that soon there will be little option but to cut back on inputs to, and outputs from, human activities. I briefly sketch some suggestions for specific solutions and new general directions. I do not propose a reversion to centralised socialist or social democratic models of the past, although I believe we can draw substantially upon them. Nor do I propose a return to a pre-industrial order, though I do suggest that we should use the best that era had to offer and revive appropriate traditions.

My alternative model is more complex than this. It involves a new four-tiered sustainability framework within which all future societies must seek to exist, but into which a number of models may fit. I propose what I call, tentatively, a 'green-red' model, which combines the virtues of environmentalism and socialism, which retains much of the decentralism now emerging in both the East and the West and which greatly modifies the machine-chemical economy without entirely abandoning all the industrial or technological aspects of modernity. 'Green-red' models (there can be many variants) will need to be more flexible, small-scale, decentralist, conservationist, cultural, traditionalist and spiritual than socialism has hitherto been. This will mean a greening of the red. Both 'greens' and 'reds' should then seek to replace unsustainable industrial capitalism with 'green-red' models for a less growth-obsessed, globalised, materialistic economy and for a more just, traditionalist, culturally-oriented, ecologically and socially sustainable world order.

2   THE BLUE OVER GREEN POLITICS

ONE of the verities of politics is that for every successful political action there is an opposite, though not necessarily equal, reaction. For some years the inflating balloon of 'green politics' has floated so confidently over the Australian polity that attempts to burst it were inevitable. The most publicised shot so far was on 1 November 1989 when the then primary industry minister, John Kerin, condemned 'competitive environmentalism' and 'sanctimonious' behaviour by political parties and governments as they clamour for the environmental vote (Kerin, 1989:5). This was widely reported as a snipe at the Hawke Government's alleged pro-green opportunism and knuckling under to a pressure group. Soon after, Kerin was backed by Labor Senate leader, John Button, some Government back-benchers and sundry commentators around the country. The era of green political battlefields had begun. Environmentalists were variously accused of using distorted arguments, exaggerated claims and hysteria, of having an 'against everything' mentality, of being cupboard socialists, economic saboteurs, and new religious zealots, and even of being unethical or creating a 'Big Green Lie'.[3]

Kerin acknowledged that 'the sins of the past are now being visited upon us' and that any government not 'conservation minded and environmentally aware is crazy', but he warned that as a small trading country we must 'deal with the mainstream against the harsh reality of international competitiveness (sic)' (Kerin 1989:4 and 6). So environmental purity must be traded against economic prosperity. One business spokesman said that some green assertions were true but solutions were only possible through sustainable development (i.e. growth) because 'Poverty is toxic to the environment' (Wallis, 1989). New Right spokesman Des Moore claimed that greens ignore the national interest and that 'whichever environmental problems prove to be real', they will be solved by growth and technology (letter to *Age*, 6 November 1989). One banker said that banks are losing interest in lending where an environmental dispute is likely (ABC News, 21 May 1990), and some banks are now thought to be reducing their lending in Australia for this reason.

The NSW Greiner Liberal Government, fearing that Labor may have appropriated the 'green middle ground', is aiming to attract and reinforce the apparent majority who still worry more about the economy and local issues such as parks or garbage than about global environmental problems. Greiner has criticised the 'dreams of Utopian idealists' and is following market-based measures mapped out by New Right think tanks.[4] There are plenty of genuinely concerned politicians, but most public figures have discovered the 1987 Brundtland Report (WCED, 1990) which, while warning about all manner of global disasters impending, has managed to still recommend continued growth. Unions have gradually shifted from hostility towards 'greenies', especially where their activities seemed to threaten jobs, to support for campaigns against health-threatening pollution. Union leaders often hint that greens lack economic perspectives and flexibility, but support their general claims (eg. Ogden, *Arena* 87, 1989). In 1989 the ACTU dropped its 60-year old pro-development policy and added a mild environmental plank to its platform.

A litmus test for the blue over green politics was the March 1990 federal election in which environmental and conservation issues played a major role. Democrats, Greens and other independents received an unprecedented vote of around 17 per cent, while the Greens' tally of 10 per cent or more in parts of WA and NSW helped Labor win or hold several seats. Greens claim that they were directly responsible for a national primary vote swing of 2.5 per cent, although political scientists put it at about one per cent.[5] Such figures compare favourably with the performance of Green Parties in Europe, while the Green vote in the 1989 Tasmanian State election of about 18 per cent was one of the highest in the world. Opinion polls have found 87 per cent of Australians concerned about the environment, only 11 per cent believing 'too much fuss' is made of it, 61 per cent opposing mining in national parks, 70 per cent favouring trees over jobs, 78 per cent wanting forests conserved (this figure being even higher for women and young people), 93 per cent wanting stronger environmental action and 96 per cent wanting animal and plant species protected.[6] The age of green politics is here to stay, although these figures suggest that green attitudes might not coalesce into support for political movements based solely on environmental issues. Issue-based polls show a majority of people still ranking the economy as more important than the environment, but the occasional study now shows the reverse (eg. *Age*, 15 June 1990:22).

Environmentalists may at times be over-zealous and their economic arguments may be poorly constructed at present, as their detractors often claim, but many accusations against them are false. The environment is certainly not a recent, hyped-up, single issue campaign, but a plea over very real inter-related issues. The claim by cynics that 'greenies' are yuppies with vested ideological interests is nonsense (see O'Connor in *AFR* 23 August 1990). In any case, most industrialists are from middle and upper classes. Environmental concerns now cut across all classes, one UK survey finding minimal differences among five broad occupational groupings. Professionals were more inclined to worry about chemicals or nuclear wastes and workers about noise, ugly buildings or dog droppings, but the difference was only marginal. Unskilled workers showed the highest level of concern about wildlife destruction of all classes in the survey. In fact many studies indicate that working class people may suffer more from environmentally-related illnesses than the more affluent. A recent Victorian study has shown that people in the inner and western suburbs of Melbourne suffer well above average rates of cancer, respiratory problems and circulatory disorders, all of which have known environmental links.[7]

Some environmental activists are government-funded, but grants are miniscule compared with the over $1000 m annually provided for industry assistance. Many environmentalists work voluntarily for a cause they see as vital, and this form of commitment cannot be compared, as it sometimes falsely is, with the vested interests companies have in promoting development. There are now some 2,500 environment-related groups in Australia with over 400,000 members, many more than belong to political parties (Kerin, 1989:7). World-wide environmentalism may be one of the largest social movements in history. The Greens' success reflects rather than leads this awareness.

It may be true, as some commentators assert, that environmentalists use emotional appeals and 'symbol-wielding power', but terms like 'religious zeal', 'chilling idealism' or 'romanticism' are inappropriate.[8] The arguments of the environmental movements are generally empirical, which makes it the first movement in history to raise millenarian-like claims on a scientific basis. Some strategists within the Labor Party still think the government has been conned by 'greenies' (*Age*, 3 September 90) and that the environment should be down-graded, for electoral purposes, in favour of a better economic performance. Given the polling evidence, however, such advice seems unwise, and it should not be assumed that the two concerns are always mutually exclusive. In my view, the Labor Government's economic dilemmas are largely due to its hasty adoption of New Right economic policies and to excessive integration into the global capitalist economy. More importantly, however, I will argue in the following chapters that, for reasons of both principle and practice, environmental considerations will have to become more central to economic policy-making.

3 THE GREAT DEBATE

IT is commonly suggested by non-green writers, both Right and Left, that environmental concerns are of recent vintage and are secondary to traditional needs such as food, clothing, shelter, education, welfare, equality and social justice. But Plato's description of soil erosion in early Greece (Quotation 1) and records of pollution even in Biblical times demonstrate that the problem of relations between humans and Nature is a long-standing and fundamental one. There is archeological evidence that some earlier societies collapsed because of ecological damage to their agricultural systems (Simmons, 1989). Environmentalists today would argue that ecological problems affect all the above-mentioned traditional needs so that environmental matters are integral to society not just supplementary luxuries.

It could be argued that an environmentalist stream of thought, a green option, has always existed alongside mainstream philosophies. There have always been advocates of greater harmony with Nature, though the idea of human domination over Nature has gradually taken precedence as a rationale for capitalist industrialism and resource-intensive development.[9] Nineteenth century conservationists such as John Muir and G. P. Marsh in the US, or Sir Albert Howard in the UK, foresaw clashes between Nature and emerging industrial development patterns. Their actions led to organic agriculture movements and to national parks. Since 1960 there have been three waves of green debates, those of the mid-1960s and early 1970s being diverted by more immediate economic exigencies. The third began around 1988 with striking, fresh evidence on issues such as global warming, and has led to a new round of policy promises by governments.

Within this great continuing debate the so-called 'pessimists' believe that industrial development has vast uncounted costs in terms of innumerable pollutants, depletion of non-renewable resources, mismanagement of renewable resources (forests, fisheries, etc.), undue reliance on non-renewable energy sources and excessive population growth. Economists such as Boulding and Georgescu-Roegen pointed out that the Earth was a 'spaceship' dependent wholly on its inherited materials plus sunlight. Energy and matter are subject to increasing 'entropy' or dispersion to an unsuitable form. This means that the universe is running down and resources are on a one way path to obliteration, as in Georgescu-Roegen's non-invertable hourglass (Quotation 5, Box 1). Associated problems include population, soil erosion, species destruction, decline of cultures, urban congestion, individual alienation and many more. People holding such views have been called 'pessimists' because they hold that 'exponential' (accelerating) population and economic growth will deplete resources and the environment faster than we expect. The famous *Limits To Growth* report (Meadows, 1972) projected 'eco-catastrophe', or a collapse of the Earth's carrying capacity, around the middle of the next century. Though often accused of doom-mongering, many environmentalists actually believe such a fate can be avoided by a change in direction, but they mostly think that continued industrial growth is unsustainable and that the dream of fabulous wealth for all is fantasy.

During each wave 'pessimists' have been answered by 'optimists' or expansionists (my term) who claim that the evidence points to plentiful resources and declining pollution. The latter argue that the free market can switch to substitutes as required and find new resource-saving, pollution-abating technologies. The best known pioneer 'optimists' were the late Herman Kahn and his colleagues at the Hudson Institute in the US. They suggested that population would stabilise at 15 to 30 billion sometime next century or the one after, with economic growth levelling out at per capita incomes vastly higher than today. Even the poorest pygmy in Africa will be watching Dallas and driving a BMW. The world will bask in the glory of the ultimate achievement — a US upper middle class lifestyle. If necessary, we can sift the seas, mine the Moon and catch asteroids for extra resources. Most 'optimists' accept the notion of eventual limits to growth, but with the market easing us into it, and they advocate growing for as long as possible. Beckerman once spoke of growth continuing for at least the next 2,500 years, a view which even most 'optimists' would now regard as nonsense. Most non-greens, Right, Left and mainstream, interpret Plato (Quotation 1, Box 1) to mean that human activities necessarily impinge on the environment and have done so throughout history. To pollute is to be human. It is a trade-off between purity and comfort. This is not very helpful, however, because there are various development strategy options, some much more environmentally damaging than others. Environmentalists believe that optimists are largely ignorant of ecological realities.[10]

An old adage has it that a pessimist is a well informed optimist, but these terms are no longer appropriate in the environmental context, however, as there are now so many streams of thought. For general reference to views on the above-mentioned issues I will use the terms 'expansionist', 'precautionist' and 'conservator', as explained in the Preface. Given that all streams accept an eventual end to growth, the issues today involve questions such as — when will the slow-down begin?, can growth really alleviate poverty?, to what extent must we consider future generations?, how much human impact can the Earth absorb?, how much diversity of species must be maintained?, what trade-offs are available?, and what new policy systems are required?

Socialist doctrines too can arguably claim an antique lineage, but modern socialism is largely a product of the Industrial Revolution and the social damage it caused rather than reaction to its impact on Nature, though some pioneer socialists worried about that as well (Quotation 3, Box 1). Nineteenth century socialists were primarily concerned about class bifurcation, poverty, social inequity and injustice, worker alientation and the lack of social amenities under industrial capitalism. They sought solutions in redistribution of property and income, public welfare and education, active state intervention and worker organisation, although industrial growth struck them as appropriate, especially for raising all living standards, if properly regulated by the state. Most socialists claimed to be espousing a complete social doctrine rather than just a special interest as 'naturists' were thought to be doing. In time many sub-streams sprang forth, but it is useful to distinguish four major streams, of which the first two are the most predominant:

i   those whose first priority was for worker organisations to overthrow capitalism and establish a more equitable form of socialist industrial growth (notably the Marxists);

ii   those who wanted worker and other popular movements to democratically reform or transform capitalism via the state in order that the product of industrial growth be more equitably distributed between people and between the public and private sectors (notably the Saint Simonians and later the Fabians);

iii   those who wanted revolution or radical reform to overthrow both capitalism and much or all of the state structure, replacing these with semi-autonomous communities and direct worker-control of industrial enterprises (notably the Anarchists and Guild Socialists);

iv   those who saw at least some of the fault in industrialism itself and wanted some degree of modification to its main features and impacts, along with the overthrow or reform of capitalism (notably Ruskin, Morris and Tawney — Quotations 3 and 4 — as well as some Anarchists such as Kropotkin).

Although growth and reform have alleviated some of the problems which worried early socialists, many problems remain, or have even been exacerbated by the rise of the New Right. Socialist solutions remain relevant to social problems, but traditional socialist frameworks must now be modified to deal with additional problems bequeathed to us by the twentieth century, particularly the environmental crisis. Socialist responses may have to shift to the traditions of the fourth stream and away from the others which have hitherto predominated. The next chapter will examine the main problems with which we are now faced.

Box 2   Some Definitions of Sustainable Development

1. Sustainable development is development that meets the needs of the present without compromising the ability of future generations to meet their own needs (WCED, 1990:87).

2. In essence, sustainable development is a process of change in which the exploitation of resources, the direction of investments, the orientation of technological development and institutional change are all in harmony and enhance both current and future potential to meet human needs and aspirations (WCED, 1990:90).

3. Sustainable development will be facilitated by a diverse and flexible economy which is able to withstand internal and external shocks. Such an economy needs investment in capital, skills, research, and in the case of new sources of raw materials, exploration and sustainable development of new sources or substitutes ... (Commonwealth, 1990:4).

4. ... our duty is not to turn our backs on economic development but to ensure that our use of resources is efficient, and that we provide future generations with the greatest range of options to satisfy their wants. This cannot be achieved without economic growth — which provides the savings and technological progress necessary to combine growth with high environmental standards. Poverty and poor economic performance are themselves toxic to the environment (BCA, 1990:7).

5. The whole approach to sustainable development must be market or demand driven, after careful appraisal of the international or global context. The fundamental approach taken is that market demand will be generated world wide as the standards of living in the underdeveloped countries and in the developed countries expands (Australian Paper Manufacturers, cited in Crawford et al, 1991:6).

6. (Sustainable development) … requires a shift in the balance of the way economic progress is pursued. Environmental concerns must be properly integrated into economic policy … The environment must be seen as a valuable, frequently essential input to human wellbeing (Pearce et al, 1989:XIV).

7. Ecological sustainability emphasises the qualitative aspect of development, as opposed to the more traditional emphasis on quantitative growth (Hare, 1990:5).

8. The sustainable society is one that lives within the self-perpetuating limits of its environment. That society … is not a 'no-growth' society … (but) recognises the limits of growth … (and) looks for alternative ways of growing (James Coomer cited in Pearce, et al 1989:175).

9. Sustainability requires that the organisation of all human systems and the equitable fulfilment of basic human needs be done in a manner which ensures the survival of all other species and the maintenance of ecosystems in the very long-term (my preferred definition).

4 SUSTAINABILITY AND LIMITS TO GROWTH

THE current fashion amongst governments, policy advisers and economists throughout the world is the view that the environment can be integrated with the economy and reconciled with growth via 'sustainable development' (SD). To date the notion is only vaguely formulated and begs questions about the type of economy which might tailor with the environment. Mainstream environmental economists say that the economy and the environment must be married by the market economy providing the correct 'signals', while many socialists want marriage by the transition from capitalism to a more planned socialism, shorn of monopoly and TNCs. Even many 'realistic' environmentalists now aver that some growth, via re-vamped industry, can be made compatible with the most urgent environmental requirements. In this chapter I seek to shed doubt on these claims by arguing that the mechanisms upon which they rest are less reliable than expansionists assume, that the environmental crisis is more serious than many people acknowledge, that there are more limits to growth than is generally realised and that current SD models are inadequate for permanent solutions. If the economy is to marry the environment on its own terms, it may turn out to be a shotgun wedding.

• DEFINING SUSTAINABLE DEVELOPMENT — AS YOU LIKE IT!

The terms 'sustainable development' and 'sustainability' appeared in the late 1960s, were popularised by the 1972 UN Stockholm Conference, the 1980 World Conservation Strategy and the 1987 UN-appointed World Commission of Environment and Development (WCED, 1990), and are sure to be the buzz words of the 1990s. The WCED's various definitions of SD (1 and 2 in Box 2) are the most quoted at present, and the WCED report has been popular because it managed to combine strong warnings about ecological dangers with advocacy of a 'a new era of growth' which is to be 'forceful and at the same time socially and environmentally sustainable' (WCED, 1990:xvi).

Pearce et al (1989) have explained current SD proposals as complementarity between economic growth and the environment (PW in Box 3) rather than the trade-off (MC in Box 3) which characterises current development models. The latter, which I call 'machine-chemical models' and which still predominate in industrial societies, see environmental, social or cultural damage as the 'price of economic progress', a notion which is increasingly being seen as unsustainable (Quotations 6 and 7, Box 1). By contrast, the complementarity approach (PW in Box 3) advocated by Pearce et al (1989), the WCED (1990) and others is based on a development model which integrates environmental factors into economic decision-making and thereby is allegedly sustainable, although it must be fostered by government. I will hereinafter refer to this approach as the 'Pearce-WCED model.'

Unfortunately the details of this model are sketchy and there are imponderables about the concepts behind the diagram in Box 3, such as how GDP is measured, how environmental quality is defined and how we identify the SD path. These uncertainties have enabled many dubious perceptions of SD to flourish. For instance, the current Australian Government uses the popular WCED definition of SD (Definition 1, Box 2) and espouses many aspects of the Pearce-WCED model, but also emphasises growth, resource development and resilience which reinforce the

Box 3 Relation Between GDP Growth and Environmental Quality Under Three Development Models

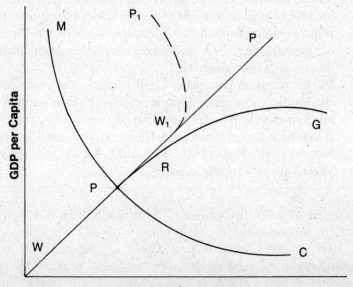

Source: Adapted from Pearce et al, 1989: Box 1.6, p.20.

- MC is the relationship between growth and the environment under the machine-chemical model (whether of the capitalist or socialist variety), with its heavy dependence on capital, chemicals, energy and non-renewable resources. There is a trade-off between the two, with environmental deterioration seen as the price of 'progress'. Among those who accept that there must be a trade-off, expansionists seek the high growth end of the curve while conservators seek the high environmental quality end.
- PW is the relationship which Pearce and the WCED claim would prevail under their SD model, with increasing levels of both growth and environmental quality being possible for a long time yet. I am sceptical

and consider that the relationship under the Pearce-WCED model would be more like $P_1 W_1$ with an eventual trade-off.

- GR is the likely relationship under my proposed alternative 'green-red' model, which involves a levelling out of growth, in the not-too-distant future, at some optimum point, but with continuing environmental improvement. Beyond that point growth will stabilitse, or perhaps in 'over-developed' societies even turn downwards for a time (NEG).

- In this diagram per capita GDP is used as a proxy for the notion of material economic growth. Environmental quality is to be interpreted broadly.

- If at present all machine-chemical economics are around point P, then MC, PW and GR represent three alternative development paths.

Government's established policies (Definition 3, Box 2). Likewise, Australian business interests also tend to use WCED definitions and then proceed to interpret these as meaning growth, competitiveness, marketing or other 'business as usual' propositions (Definitions 4 and 5, Box 2). Commonwealth environment minister Ros Kelly, has accused business of using SD to justify 'unrestrained development' (quoted in *AFR* editorial, 5 September 1990).

The SD debate has, therefore, been too generalised to resolve fundamental differences. Although most governments and industrialists now proclaim complementarity between the machine-chemical economy and the environment, a trade-off relationship is still implicit in the views of many expansionists, such as those Australian business groups which suggest that development is not possible without some loss of species and ecological damage, or that development is hampered because over a quarter of the country is 'locked up' in Aboriginal reserves, heritage areas or conservation zones. Some common assertions by Australian businessmen today are that we must shift from environmental protection to 'environmental management'; that we should seek to preserve only 'important' species; that stability and resilience of environments should be the main criteria for

SD, rather than 'preservation', because ecosystems are always changing anyway; and that an efficient, competitive, technologically dynamic economy is a prerequisite for solving environmental problems.[11] Such views imply, whether acknowledged or not, a trade-off between economy and environment and a preference for the upper end of the MC curve (Box 3).

Most expansionists regard Nature as niggardly and to be improved upon by technology and growth, which are assumed to be prerequisites for solutions to environmental damage. Conservators, by contrast, object to the notion that environmental problems should be subject to 'after the fact' solutions, holding instead that sound ecosystems are a prerequisite for development and that protection should be built in from the outset. Conservators see the environment as crucial to life, not just 'valuable' (vidé Pearce — Definition 6, Box 2) or 'aesthetic' (vidé Davidson, *Age*, 11 October 1990), let alone an optional extra or a luxury good as it is often implicitly seen. Conservators believe that Nature has provided everything required for a good, modest life-style, albeit unevenly spread, so long as we protect Her and recognise that many economic activities can seriously hurt Her (Suzuki, 1990a and b). This implies some trade-off and a preference for the lower end of the MC curve (Box 3), although many conservators may wish ultimately to shift to a different curve. Some 'realistic' conservators now accept the complementarity curve (PW in Box 3) of the Pearce-WCED model, but prefer that the term SD be prefaced with 'ecological' and advocate a more qualitative form of growth based on services, selected high technology, energy conservation and so forth (Definition 7, Box 2). Others, however, fear that excessive liberties are being taken with the SD concept and want it abandoned (eg. Suzuki, 1990 b).

In sum, although governments and expansionist commentators are currently paying much lip service to the SD concept, few appear to have grasped that the Pearce-WCED model requires a drastic change of growth-development path and even fewer have made moves in that direction. In the following sub-sections I seek to show that many of the systems which make up our current growth-development path are unsustainable, as the WCED itself has suggested (Quotations 6 and 7, Box 1), and that the prospects for future growth are limited by a much wider range of factors than is generally realised.

Expansionists and most precautionists base their optimism for the prospects of continued 'clean' growth on four key inter-linked propositions — i. that markets can facilitate the necessary adjustments; ii. that technological solutions will normally be found; iii. that resource and energy throughput can be 'de-coupled' from output (a concept I will refer to as 'RETP de-coupling'), meaning that certain technologies will enable output to grow without greatly increasing RETP; iv. that plenitude can be perpetuated and equity for future generations can be maintained by ensuring that depletion of natural capital *in* the ground is compensated for with construction of an equivalent amount of human-made capital *on* the ground; some call this 'constant wealth', but as constancy is problematic I call it the 'capital compensation process'. I argue that optimism based on these propositions is fundamentally flawed. In addition, I argue that because Pearce and the WCED also rely substantially on the first three of these propositions (they have a much improved version of the fourth) their SD path too is flawed, if less fundamentally so. I then propose an alternative approach to sustainability.

• ANYHOW, HAVE A MINERAL — NON-RENEWABLE RESOURCES

In 1972 Meadows et al stunned a still growing and complacent world by claiming that exhaustion of many non-renewable resources (metals and minerals) would, by next century, be placing severe limits on growth prospects. Critics attacked the authors for allegedly using obsolete data, for neglecting adaptive mechanisms (see below) and generally for being doomsters. While accepting that exponential growth could theoretically bring exhaustion, expansionists argue that this will not happen in practice because of four key factors and adaptive mechanisms:

i. estimates of reserves are unreliable because search may not be undertaken until a need is foreseen;

ii. 'backstop' resources are available in the form of some twenty 'super-abundant' metals (iron, aluminium, etc.) of which there are probably vast reserves in the Earth's crust, the oceans, Antarctica, the Moon, asteroids and so on;

iii. markets will always translate scarcities into price rises sufficiently to induce new supplies from higher-cost sites, from the substitution of other materials and from recycling, or through some combination of these;

iv. technological innovation will provide alternatives to natural resources (eg. synthetics and electronics) or ways to economise on resource usage, thus 'de-coupling' production from metal and mineral inputs. Some go as far as to assert that all this could almost completely 'liberate' us from raw materials, allowing residual resources to last forever.[12]

An example of these claims is the authoritative case study of copper by Gordon et al (1987) which purportedly demonstrates that copper could be 90 per cent replaced by substitutes (aluminium, titanium, steel, glass and plastic) or by new technologies (optical fibre, ceramics, etc.), with the other ten per cent of copper requirements being supplied from low grade ores, the mining of rubbish tips, recycling and so on. But Gordon et al conceded that supplies of the best copper could be exhausted by as early as 2070, less than a century from now.

I argue that there are fundamental flaws in this story. First, although extensive new supplies of many resources have been discovered and estimates of reserves greatly raised since Meadows et al wrote, these will only sustain a few more decades of growth when rates of growth are 'exponential' — i.e. the rate of increase is increasing. This will be especially so if Third World countries industrialise at rates the WCED and other expansionists are urging.[13] Yet it remains hypothetical whether we could, or even should, try to tap the so-called 'super-abundant' resources which expansionists see everywhere, or whether it would be energy-efficient to do so (see Gever et al, 1986:Ch.2).

Second, the resource price slumps since 1972 have mostly been due to recessions and the widespread use of energy subsidies, rather than to the elimination of scarcity as many expansionists claim (Gever et al, 1986:96ff). Also, some resources have been in over-supply due to panic exploration after the Meadows et al report, and this has temporarily weakened prices. Exploration costs are likely to rise rapidly next century (Goodland and Ledec, 1987:39) and large resource price rises have been forecast, copper by a factor of sixty, for instance (Gordon et al, 1987). Even if resource prices do rise in future, it is not clear that expanionists' faith in the ability of markets to reflect scarcity is warranted. Most indicators of scarcity are unreliable (Brown and Field in Smith, 1979) and prices may remain stable until markets perceive near-exhaustion. Current prices are based on flows rather than stocks and so may not be sensitive to in-ground scarcities. Futures markets have the same limitations and some economists admit that they are not the answer (eg. Solow, 1974).

Third, the key process of RETP de-coupling, or 'de-materialisation' as some call it, is problematic. Some believe that de-coupling has been responsible for the recent weak resource demand and prices, which have adversely affected trade balances of resource exporting countries such as Australia. Others, however, suggest that demand and price trends are subject to a number of statistical illusions, are cyclically related and have risen with economic recovery in the late 1980s. Some studies suggest that de-coupling is clearer in the US than in most other countries, that it is only pronounced for a small number of metals, that metals intensity (metal usage per unit of output) is actually increasing at present and that many of the efficiencies which have reduced intensity are just 'one-off' savings.[14] Many of the new technologies thought capable of RETP de-coupling might likewise be limited in their capacity to do so because some materials will always be required, and computers, for instance, have actually increased paper usage ten-fold, not reduced it as some predicted.[15] The notion that efficiencies and technologies can ultimately 'liberate' us from resource inputs is probably closer to science fiction than fact.[16]

Fourth, the prospects for perpetual recycling are also problematic. Recycling technologies are improving, but collection is difficult, markets for recycled materials are sluggish and where recycling infrastructure has been established, particularly in the US, it can also raise demand for new materials to maintain feedstock. There are limits to how often material can be recycled, some matter is lost in recycling and certain recycling processes require much energy or cause substantial pollution. Many economists erroneously believe that matter is constant and can be transformed at will or recycled forever (eg. Thurow, 1981:111), but in fact matter, like energy, is entropic and eventually disappears down Georgescu-Roegen's non-invertible hour glass (Quotation 5, Box 1).

Finally, many expansionists base their optimism on forecasts which foresee no shortages for the next fifty years, and most refuse to look beyond that span because of the uncertainties allegedly involved. But this does not mean that there will not be shortages soon after that time-frame, and some more far-sighted economists now concede that certain resources will be exhausted within a century or so (eg. Ayers and Kneese, 1989). If this proves correct we will have wolfed the world's best resources in less than two centuries of the machine-chemical development model. Many expansionists are actually saying, irresponsibly in my view, that future generations must look after themselves. In sum, I suggest that those who believe mechanisms such as market adaptation, RETP de-coupling or recycling will enable resources to last more or less forever are over-optimistic and perhaps deluded.

• BOWSER BOOZERS ANONYMOUS — ENERGY

In 1972 Meadows et al foresaw a life of only 20 years for petroleum stocks and 111 years for coal. Today an emerging consensus view has oil reserves levelling out by early next century, gas in 200 years and coal in 3,000 years at current consumption rates, although there are shorter estimates, and the most optimistic projection for oil is near-exhaustion by 2080. Australia's energy life-spans are put at 11 years for oil, gas 63, uranium 124, black coal 263 and brown coal 1,144.[17]

Expansionists' arguments regarding future energy supplies and the mechanisms involved are similar to those regarding minerals, and similar criticisms thus apply. Expansionists suggest that our plentiful coal stocks can serve as a 'backstop' while nuclear, renewable and other sources are developed and while technology de-couples production from energy inputs, thus reducing the ratio of energy to GDP. However, there are many problems with this story. First, energy usage is 'price inelastic', so that future price rises may not greatly reduce demand, induce efficiencies or encourage alternatives as expansionist free market theorists expect (see Gever et al, 1986:22ff). Second, a fifth of all energy production is wasted, especially because of the extreme energy inefficiency of electricity generation, and there may be limits to the capacity of technology to reduce the wastage factor (Gever et al, 1986:101ff).

Third, most economists overlook the fact that it takes energy to obtain new energy supplies. The surplus obtained is sometimes called the 'energy profit ratio' and a ratio of less than one indicates a nett loss of energy in the process. A study by Gever et al (1986:Ch.2) has found that from early ratios of up to 100 for some fuels, the ratios for most US energy sources are now less than ten and already less than one for a few. Gever et al think that ratios for 'hard path' fuels (non-renewables, nuclear, etc.) will continue to decline, thus rendering some anticipated options non-viable.

Fourth, the world's heavy reliance on fossil fuels is thought to be the main cause of rising carbon dioxide levels and the resultant global warming (see below). Present indications are that it will never be technically possible to prevent substantial carbon dioxide emissions from coal combustion (Saddler in ANU, 1990:187).

Fifth, although some de-coupling is occurring and since the first oil crisis most industrial countries have reduced their ratios of energy to GDP/GNP (ranging from Japan's 31 per cent to a modest six per cent in Australia and Canada), there are signs that this declining trend is levelling out, especially as oil prices fall. Conservation in some sectors is often counteracted by an energy-using bias in others (eg. in some high technology sectors and in agriculture), or by general demand expansion. Only a few OECD countries have achieved an absolute decline in energy consumption to date. Sweden has all but abandoned an earlier target of zero energy growth by the 1990s, while Australia maintains one of the highest energy growth rates in the world.[18] Despite this, and despite the view of one prominent energy consultant that Australia's energy-use pattern is unsustainable (Saddler in ANU, 1990), the Hawke Government anticipates an expansion of energy-intensive industries and greatly increased transportation by the next century (Hawke, 1989), while business groups have rejected energy-saving measures currently being proposed by environmentalists (*Age*, 19 August 1991). There is now almost overwhelming evidence that energy conservation is the cheapest, most efficient and most environmentally sound way of dealing with energy problems (see Lovins in Leggett, 1990), but it would require major changes in infrastructure, consumer behaviour, government policy and rectification of market imperfections (see Saddler in ANU, 1990), hence this solution is dumped into the 'too hard' basket.

Sixth, conventional 'hard' technological solutions such as coal liquefaction, nuclear power, breeder reactors and fusion are extremely costly and many entail massive environmental risks. Environmentally-sympathetic 'energy optimists' (my term) such as Lovins and Goldemberg (in Leggett, 1990) believe that the whole world can achieve 'rich country' living standards by next century through concerted energy conservation and new 'soft' (renewable) energy systems. Certainly many of these innovations seem promising (eg. a house run on human body heat) but governments obsessed with growth and 'big' systems are still expanding most 'hard' energy systems while reducing research on renewables. In Australia we spend over 25 times as much on nuclear research as on renewables, even though our prospects for solar, wind and tidal sources are thought to be very good.[19]

Finally, energy has a special role in the universe, for it derives solely from the stars (our Sun), is subject to entropy and once used is lost down Georgescu-Roegen's non-invertible hour glass (Quotation 5, Box 1). Traditional societies used energy moderately and their agriculture, for instance, produced ten or more times the energy it used. By contrast, most industrial systems are massive energy users and our machine-chemical agriculture can use 10 to 100 times more energy than it produces. We are the first society in history to construct systems which require far more energy than is ready at hand. We now use fossil fuel 10,000 times faster than it is forming and consume in a year what took Nature a million years to create. Such patterns are clearly unsustainable in the long-term, which suggests the need for a shift, as soon as practicable, to concerted conservation, renewable energy sources and predominantly organic agriculture.[20]

• TRAGIC COMMONS — RENEWABLE RESOURCES

Resources such as forests, fisheries, soils and water are theoretically renewable, but they have usage limitations and can be mismanaged. Often they must be used communally and so risk competitive over-exploitation, which US biologist, Garrett Hardin, has called the 'tragedy of the commons'. The state of these resources today is widely regarded as parlous. Many of the world's fisheries have experienced periodic collapses (UNEP, 1987: Table 3.10), some 95 per cent of the world fish catch is from over-fished zones and much of it is threatened by pollution (WCED, 1990:307). Timber resources are being plundered at a rate that will almost eliminate tropical moist forests early next century. Countries such as Australia and the US are said to have nett timber increases through re-planting, but this is disputed, and replacement involves monocultural plantations compared with the richly varied ecosystems of natural forests. Acid rain and other pollutants are now causing massive damage to forests and reducing crop yields in all parts of the world, while deforestation is seriously damaging water catchment areas (Brown in Brown, 1991).

Water usage in Europe and Asia is expected to rise from ten per cent of run-off now to 20-25 per cent by the end of the century (WCED, 1990:76). Supplies are near-exhaustion in parts of western USA where some governments have planned to deplete their water allocations in 25 to 50 years, a clear case of Hardin's thesis and of unsustainable development. Severe local water shortages are common in the Third World, while regional and inter-country conflicts over water supplies are looming in India and the Middle East (Shiva, 1989: Starr in *GW*, 24 March 1991:19). At present Australia technically uses less than ten per cent of run-off, but the story is complex and uncertain. Victoria, for instance, currently uses about 20 per cent of run-off, but the feasible usage limit may be less than 30 per cent, so that perhaps more than two thirds of ultimate capacity is now being utilised. Melbourne faces water shortages within a decade. Usage imbalance is enormous, the USA using 70 times more water per capita than

Ghana, for instance, and water is thought to be seriously under-priced in most countries.[21]

The world now averages one dam burst per year (WCED, 1990:238), and there is mounting evidence that large dams are disruptive, ecologically disastrous, of dubious value relative to smaller traditional supply systems and are often rendered ineffective due to silting. World-wide popular resistance to large dams and other 'hard' technologies is growing. Water supplies in all parts of the world are seriously contaminated from industrial and agricultural chemicals, including in the USA where 40 per cent of groundwater is polluted. Some 40,000 children die daily from lack of water or from disease borne in contaminated water supplies, and by 2000 some 40 per cent of Africans will be at risk in this way. The water contamination problem has been referred to as a 'time bomb'. Some estimates suggest that at current usage rates global water supplies could support 20 billion people, but far fewer if usage accelerates and contamination levels worsen.[22]

Another time bomb is soil degradation, especially in the forms of topsoil loss, nutrient depletion, salinity and desertification. As much as a third of the Earth's land surface may now be affected and rich countries are not exempt. The causes are numerous, but particularly significant are deforestation, irrigation, chemical farming, monoculture and perhaps even ploughing. Data are unreliable as yet but in the US declines in agricultural productivity of up to two per cent per annum have been recorded in some areas, and this could reach ten per cent next century. Half the world's croplands are losing topsoil at rates which will reduce long-term productivity.[23] China now admits that a third of all cultivated land and a quarter of all grasslands are degraded (Li, 1990:18).

Over half of Australia's farm land is salinated or otherwise degraded and up to two thirds (80 per cent in NSW) needs some restoration. Some ten per cent of cropland and 25 per cent of pastures may have already been destroyed beyond repair. Over $1 b in soil nutrients are lost annually in grain exports, monocultural wheat cropping being especially harsh on soils. One loaf of bread uses seven kilos of topsoil. All this is costing at least $600 m per annum in production losses and would take a minimum of $2 b to rectify. The extent of land degradation both in Australia and world-wide is staggering and is still not fully grasped by the public. Commonwealth Treasurer, John Kerin, has claimed that most Australian agriculture is sustainable, but many disagree (eg. Squires in ANU, 1990) and the WCED (1990:96-7) has hinted that large-scale commercial agriculture may not be a sustainable option for developing countries. I suggest that in fact machine-chemical agriculture in general is not sustainable and that modern versions of traditional organic methods must be sought.[24]

Perhaps the most serious resource problem of all is that we are now destroying species at rates of over 100 times the natural rates of extinction, which may be dangerously reducing the diversity required for a balanced gene pool and ecological resilience. Australia has the world's worst extinction rate for mammals — ten per cent in 200 years, five times the global average, while wiping out 97 plant species and threatening 2,000 more. We know very little about ecosystems and a species which could help cure cancer may already have been destroyed. Seed patenting and commercial control of plant breeding by large TNCs is greatly reducing the number of species in general usage. I argue that our current usage rates of, and management methods for, renewable resources are generally unsustainable and that more far-reaching institutional changes are required than most mainstream observers care to admit.[25]

• STILL THE EFFLUENT SOCIETY — POLLUTION

Amongst expansionists the assertion is frequently made that pollution in OECD countries is declining and is now generally at safe levels, while most other major environmental problems are under control. The impression usually conveyed is that on balance the back of the pollution problem has been broken by good management, co-operative industry and 'smart' technologies, and that persistence in these virtues will do the rest. This is greatly to be doubted.

Some of the more common pollutants have been reduced, but seldom to pre-1970 levels, while in many OECD countries nitrous oxides, carbon monoxide, hydrocarbons and organochlorides (from pesticides) are still rising. By far the largest reductions have been for substances such as DDT and PCBs which are banned in many Western countries. Some recent reductions have mainly been due to recession cutting output (eg. Pearce, 1987:127). Hundreds of thousands of substances are in use, and most of the 1000 or so new ones which appear annually have never been thoroughly tested. Fake test results are not unknown and much toxic material is dumped illegally — 90 per cent in the US, for instance (Day, 1989:213). OECD levels of agro-chemicals, toxic wastes, garbage, noise, household and workplace pollution, electro-magnetic radiation, some water pollutants and possibly nuclear radiation are all increasing. Pollution is still spreading to hitherto untouched waterways and coastlines, while ground-water contamination and hundreds of thousands of toxic waste sites may be lethal time bombs. Major environmental disasters have been increasing in frequency and severity (Day, 1989:195ff; UNEP, 1987:Table 9.9 and other years). Some of these trends are even worse in former Soviet-bloc countries and in the Third World. The Chinese now admit, after earlier denials, that their industrialisation frenzy is dramatically raising all forms of pollution.[26]

Official data show Australia's urban pollution at around average OECD levels and our agro-chemical usage below average (UNEP, 1987 and 1989), but one study has found us suffering higher pesticide and solvent residues than the US (*Age*, 14 November 1989). Recent Australian studies have found that Sydney beaches are a health hazard (*Age*, 5 June 1990), that Melbourne air pollution is at least 30 per cent too high (*Age*, 11 September 1990) and that there is a wide range of high pollution risks in Victoria (*Age*, 12 October 1990). Solid waste pollution is rising rapidly in all 'effluent' countries and Australia now has the dubious distinction of being the world's second largest per capita producer of rubbish after the notoriously profligate US (Button, *Age*, 15 August 1990:11).

Max Singer, Herman Kahn's successor at the Hudson Institute and a leading expansionist, asserts that the environment is improving and is not sufficiently life-threatening to warrant jeopardising growth.[27] I argue that Singer's assertion is grossly irresponsible and that the reverse is the case. The catalogue of known or likely health threats is massive and growing. Over 60 per cent of US citizens still have poor quality air (French, 1990:5) and the death toll to date may be in the hundreds of thousands (Regenstein, 1982:194). Air pollutants from cars in the US may cause 30,000 deaths per annum (WWF, 1990:115). In parts of Europe similar factors may have reduced life expectancy by as much as ten years, especially in Eastern Europe (Barnett in *Age Extra*, 9 February 1991; French in Brown, 1991). In Hungary, for instance, up to 40 per cent of the population is exposed to air and water pollution at well above acceptable international standards (WWF, 1990:90), and almost six per cent of all deaths are related to air pollution (French, 1990:5). In China urban dwellers are four to six times more likely to die of lung cancer than their rural comrades (WWF, 1990:89).

In their desperation to industrialise, countries like Taiwan and South Korea have created an environmental nightmare, including a rural 'sudden death' syndrome from agro-chemicals (Bello and Rosenfield, 1990). Such chemicals may kill 10,000 people each year throughout the Third World (WCED, 1990:170), and some estimates put this figure as high as 40,000, with up to a million people affected in some way (Day, 1989:202). The world-wide daily toll of pollution-related deaths may be equivalent to one Hiroshima — over 150,000 (Day, 1989:4).

On balance the overall problem may be getting worse, not better. Lead has been found to be a greater hazard than first thought (*Age*, 7 November 1990). Pollution causes more long-term health damage than originally believed (*Age*, 30 March 1991). Radio-activity from nuclear installations may be more common and damaging than originally thought. The 1986 Chernobyl nuclear disaster is having a greater impact than first anticipated, and the death toll may be 5,000 to 10,000 rather than the official figure of 31. A whole range of illnesses are increasing in Australia and world-wide, and medical authorities now believe that much of this is pollution-related.[28] Many scientists now think that there is no such thing as 'safe-levels' for pollutants. Anti-pollution policies and technologies are improving but the latter are better at removing particles than gasses and may have damaging by-products (French, 1990; OECD, 1989). Ironically, the day the press reported John Kerin's call to resist 'greenies', many of the same newspapers carried UN reports which warned of likely massive future health risks from global warming and ozone depletion, including respiratory diseases, malaria, eye damage and skin cancer (*Age*, 2 November 1989).

A major sleeping issue, because of the long lead times involved, is what some call a 'cancer epidemic'. Many authorities now hold that 70-90 per cent of all cancers are enviromentally-related, the main culprits being hundreds of carcinogenic industrial chemicals. Industrialists deny such claims, of course, but have admitted to at least five per cent, an important concession in itself, and have been accused of cover-ups and rigging test results, so the figure is doubtless much higher. By next century cancer is thought likely to be the main cause of death, accounting for half the total, and many of these deaths may be premature. The cancer risks have risen in all age groups not just the elderly. Recent US studies have found that only two per cent of toxic substances and 12 per cent of carcinogens are regulated, while total quantities measured have stunned authorities (*GW*, 2 April 1989). New research has also demonstrated both epidemiological and physiological links between electromagnetic radiation and cancer or other health problems. Despite uncertainties about such links technocrats still plan to blanket the Earth with computers, power lines, microwave stations and satellite signals. It is often claimed that high technologies are 'clean', but in fact the electronics industry uses up to 250 chemicals, many of them quite toxic, and spills are common. This is creating very hazardous work-places and other serious impacts in both industrialised and newly industrialising countries, so that computers themselves might be 'clean' but their production is very damaging.[29]

The most formidable problems of the 'effluent' society are the 'big three' atmospheric disturbances — acid rain, ozone depletion and global warming. Acid rain (acidification of precipitation due to air pollution) has already taken thousands of lives, caused extensive health problems, damaged over half Germany's and Switzerland's trees, 'killed' thousands of Scandinavian lakes, acidi-fied European and North American soils to as much as fifty times their natural levels, ruined historic buildings and has reduced agricultural and forestry productivity. Costs to OECD countries have been estimated at US$20 b per annum just for damage to metalwork and buildings. Several international agreements and EC resolutions aim at cuts in sulphur and nitrogen emissions of around 30 to 60 per cent, but many experts believe that cuts of up to 90 per cent are required to arrest the problem.[30]

There is now indisputable evidence of serious thinning, over many parts of the globe, in the stratospheric ozone layer which protects all life on Earth from lethal cosmic radiation. This seems to be entirely due to industrial chemicals such as CFCs. Between 1987 and 1990 a series of international protocols involving almost 100 countries agreed to completely phase out the main CFC-depleting chemicals by 2000, some (including Australia) undertaking to do so by around 1997-8 (WWF, 1990:97ff). The swift global response has been promising, but success still depends on compliance and on acceptance in the Third World. Damage will take up to a century to repair and every year's delay will extend this period by many decades. CFC-substitutes still cause some ozone depletion, may have certain side-effects and have substantial 'greenhouse' impacts.

Potentially most catastrophic of all is the global warming process, which is caused through exacerbation of the natural 'greenhouse effect' by human-induced increases in natural greenhouse gasses (GHGs) such as water vapour and carbon dioxide (from burning fossil fuels), by human-made substances such as CFCs and by deforestation. There is strong (but not quite unanimous) agreement amongst scientists that warming is occurring, is probably doing so at an unprecedented rate and is of human origin. The consensus view is that of the May 1990 report by a UN Intergovernmental Panel on Climate Change (IPCC) which concluded that global temperatures have risen by 0.3° to 0.6°C since about 1890, and which forecast a 1.3°C rise by 2020 and 3°C by 2070.

Possible consequences are unclear, but could include, within a few decades, sea level rises (from ice-melts), inundation of low-lying countries and islands, massive climate changes, ruination of agriculture in countries such as Australia and the USA, the shifting of forests, higher precipitation and more cyclones in some areas, droughts in others and a variety of unpredictable ecological problems. Claims of beneficial effects in some regions cannot be assumed to be correct. The Earth's temperature has not been 3°C higher than current levels for 125 millennia, nor 5°C higher in the past two million years, so any greater increase than this would be unprecedented for most species. It may even be uncontrollably catastrophic because positive feedbacks (eg. permafrost-melts releasing vast amounts of methane) are thought likely to greatly outweigh negative ones (Leggett, 1990; WWF, 1990:93ff).

The response has not been as heartening as that for ozone-depletion, probably because many think dramatic cuts in growth and changes to industry or consumption are required. A 1988 Toronto conference recommended 20 per cent reductions in GHGs by 2005, well below the 60 per cent cuts widely advocated by scientists as the minimum sustainable requirement, yet the US and Japan lobbied against even this much. Many governments, business people and expansionist economists remain sceptical about whether the trend is real or whether the costs of response are warranted.

One Australian businessman, Shell chief Kevan Gosper, has rejected the 'religious fervour' with which Australians believe in global warming and advocates avoidance of panic measues which may be 'very expensive in the long run'. Another Shell executive, Ian McFarlane, says that Australia's share of GHG production is too small to warrant much action. In my opinion such views are totally unacceptable. The cost of prevention may be loss of a little output, but the cost of inaction may be destruction of *life on Earth*! Australia has 0.3 per cent of the global population but produces around two per cent of all GHGs, making us among the highest per capita offenders, so inaction on our part would be inexcusable. By a bizarre contrast, one company appears to have given warming projections enough credence to suggest that Australia plan to take in 'greenhouse refugees' by about 2050.[31]

Although all conservators and most precautionists counsel immediate, strong preventative measures, expansionists are taking a 'cost-benefit analysis' approach. US economist William D. Nordhaus, for instance, has scorned calls for a 60 per cent reduction in CFCs, and has judged as unacceptable the US$300 b production losses he thinks would result from preventative measures. He has expressed a preference for adaptive measures such as sea walls or climatic engineering (eg. heat-absorbing particles, carbon-eating organisms in the oceans, etc.), even though he has admitted that the latter would raise 'profound legal, ethical and environmental issues' (*Economist*, 7 July 1990:19ff). This demonstrates the almost obsessive lengths to which expansionists would go to maintain growth and material 'standards of living'.

In Australia the Commonwealth Government has adopted the Toronto target but subject to assertion of the right to maintain its restructuring programme, transport expansion, competitiveness and growth objectives. Yet one Commonwealth Government Bureau says that we are unlikely to attain this target without an unprecedented shift away from fossil fuels, large rises in energy prices and much more government regulation.[32] Most conservators believe that similar conclusions apply to almost the full range of environmental problems, so that the current industrial system and practices cannot be sustained for much longer. From the evidence presented above, I strongly concur with this judgment.

• APOCALYPSE WHEN? — THE NEW LIMITS TO GROWTH

The foregoing sub-sections are not meant as scare-mongering, but as a measured indication of the problems we face, which in many spheres are far worse than is generally realised. Resource supplies may not be as short as Meadows et al believed in 1972, but many ecological problems may be much worse. In 1974 US conservator economist Robert Heilbroner, who was regarded at the time as a dire 'pessimist', warned of the greenhouse effect and said we had 'only' 150 years to respond. On today's evidence that guess was probably wildly optimistic. The concept of 'ecocatastrophe', or total collapse of key ecosystems, which Meadows *et al* projected for mid-twenty first century, may already be occurring in some Third World countries and certain regions of Europe. The UN estimates that there are now ten million 'environmental refugees', more than in any other refugee category, and there may soon be 50 million.

The foregoing sub-sections argued that the machine-chemical model and its acoutrements are unsustainable in many respects and so will have to change dramatically very soon. The innumerable factors causing unsustainability have been variously characterised as costs of or limits to growth. Below I identify six groups of factors and their wider implications, a greater range than is generally acknowledged in the literature. I shall follow convention by referring to these factors as 'limits' to the quantity or direction of growth, but in reality there are three differing forms — those factors which render growth undesirable because of their aesthetic or other consequences; high risk factors of uncertain consequences which may render growth inadvisable; those factors which already, or may soon, place physical limits on growth.

☐ RESOURCE LIMITS

Evidence examined earlier in this chapter suggested that future growth prospects may be limited by shortages of at least some raw materials within a century or so, by shortages or adverse environmental impacts of some energy sources within decades and perhaps already by over-usage of, and damage to, renewable resources. Markets and technologies have not been as successful at solving these problems as expansionists claim. Human activity now touches all parts of the biosphere, we use almost half the world's land surface and we have depleted seven per cent of global biomass (forests, grasses, plants, etc.) between 1870 and 1970 alone (Simmons, 1989:esp.p.256).

Recent work by Vitousek, Ehrlich and others suggests that although we only directly use four per cent of terrestrial biomass, inclusion of wastage (desertification, forest burning, urban requirements, etc.) raises the figure to an astounding 40 per cent. This would allow little more than a doubling of total resource usage, which at current growth rates will occur within 40 years, but the present world population consuming at the present US rate would require a seven-fold increase. The Vitousek *et al* estimates do not include minerals or ocean biomass (we now use three per cent of the latter), but they do indicate that growth possibilities may be seriously limited. Continued expansion may therefore result in massive forest losses, species reductions and 'wild' animals living only in zoos, all of which would be aesthetically undesirable and ecologically dangerous, while some forms of growth may soon become physically impossible.[33]

☐ ECOLOGICAL LIMITS

Ecologists have assembled strong evidence that human activity is now affecting the entire biosphere, damaging ecosystems and reducing species diversity in a way which is already cutting productivity in some sectors and is probably limiting future growth potential. Many activities are therefore probably physically unsustainable while others, such as littering, landscape despoilation, wilderness reduction and loss of some species, may be sustainable in the sense of not limiting growth, but may be both aesthetically and ecologically undesirable. Degrees of sustainability or desirability cannot be quantified, however, so there are major differences between expansionists and conservators on such matters. The latter believe that the former, especially amongst economists, engineers and industrialists, do not understand ecology or the constraints it places on the growth capacity of an economy, a view with which I concur.

Expansionists (and most precautionists) see growth as liberating us from Nature where conservators see it as alienating us from Her. Expansionists hold that 'more is better than less', whereas conservators say we can 'live better with less'. Expansionists see a 'clean' environment, and even wilderness, as just another consumer good or service, the next luxury up the 'hierarchy of needs' (eg. Thurow, 1981:Ch.5), while conservators see these as complex, inter-linked and basic to our ecological life support systems. Expansionists believe that the economy should seek to satisfy wants, not just needs (see Definition 4, Box 2) and that growth must continue until *all* wants are satiated (eg. Thurow, 1981:117). Conservators think that basic needs are readily satiated, but that further wants are artificial or 'socially constructed' and should not be pampered (see below). Economics textbooks declare that needs are limited but that wants are unlimited and resources are finite, thenceforth seeking ways to efficiently deploy as many resources as are available to meet as many wants as possible. Meeting wants is often the only rationale textbooks offer for pursuing growth.

The main difference between expansionist economists and environmentalists, is that the former see the economy as operating largely independently of natural processes whereas the latter hold that links are myriad and indissoluble. The now-infamous 1976 edition of the *Journal of Economic Literature* announced that Man (sic) 'was once totally dependent' on the environment, implying that we are no longer so. Environmentalists believe this is absurd because we are integrally inter-linked with Nature (Daly in Smith, 1979:68). Even the Pearce-WCED model holds that growth is acceptable while its impacts are within the capacity of the Earth to supply resources and absorb wastes. Ecologists, by contrast, tell us that these impacts are innumerable, often unmeasurable, may not be known in advance, can be magnified by complex ecological links and may be irreversible. Solutions may be more complex, have more side-effects and require longer lead-times than we expect. Human economic systems have a bias towards young, monocultural, open-ended ecosystems with which Nature is unfamiliar.

At present it is not possible to make accurate quantitative estimates of the extent to which environmental problems restrain growth, or will do so in future. OECD countries already spend 1-2 per cent of GDP on environmental protection, a level which some think has slightly reduced productivity growth. But many believe that environmental costs are more like 6 per cent of GDP, which would require a trebling of expenditure, about what most OECD countries spend on education, and this would be likely to measurably restrain productivity, though probably not disastrously.

The bill often suggested for environmental repair in Australia is $20 b, or five per cent of GDP — about what we now spend on health and defence combined. This, if all paid for by the government (which it should not be), would raise public expenditure to around 38 per cent GDP, about the OECD average. It would require tax increases but should be manageable. If, however, environmental costs are, or in future become, as high as the estimates of an incredible 15-17 per cent of GDP in the Soviet Union (*GW*, 7 April 1991:17), then meeting such costs would dramatically affect growth potential for a long time to come. These costs could be reduced if the expenditures helped to prevent productivity losses due to ecological damage, but only in the longer-term.

□ ECONOMIC LIMITS

A number of economic mechanisms, some connected to environmental problems, some relating to equity issues and some inherent in the growth process itself, may limit growth. Early economists, the famed 'dismal scientists', thought that growth was severely constrained by the 'Law of Diminishing Returns', though modern expansionists think that technology has largely repealed, or at least postponed, this 'Law'. Now it is generally believed that countries have growth phases, beginning with rapid growth from a low industrial base, followed by slowdown, maturity and perhaps some 'de-industrialisation' (an absolute decline in industrial employment) as low productivity services expand, and as macro problems (inflation, trade deficits, etc.) hamper stimulatory policies. Per capita GDP levels in industrial countries appear to be converging as growth leaders mature and laggards catch up.

At the micro level, and more environmentally-related, Hirsch has postulated that growth is limited by increasing competition for 'positional goods' (houses in unpolluted areas, non-crowded recreation or prestige associations), which involve relative status rather than output and thus undermine productivity. Kohr, Mishan, Sale, Schumacher (1973) and others have argued that large scale economic, urban and corporate structures entail a variety of diseconomies and social costs which gradually undermine both the possibility and desirability of continuing growth. Today 40 per cent (more on some measures) of the world's population lives in urban areas and ten per cent in large cities, so that this creeping urbanism is now rapidly absorbing land, food, firewood, energy and other resources, thus raising infrastructure and administrative costs and perhaps hindering growth. Some cities are now large enough to influence atmospheric conditions and the environment (Simmons, 1989:234). Following Schumpeter, some argue that deteriorating incentives may be reducing the dynamism of entrepreneurship, although a few economic historians now think the role of entrepreneurship in development has been over-stated.

Two equity issues, socio-economic and inter-generational equity, are crucial but neglected elements of the environmental debate. Regarding socio-economic equity, especially income distribution, three views are common. First, many mainstream economists believe that resources can be redistributed to poorer classes (via welfare) but that there is a trade-off with efficiency and so this limits growth. Second, others, including the New Right, are sceptical that resources can be deliberately redistributed and so favour continued growth to 'float all boats', thereby eliminating absolute poverty and warding off class unrest. Third, a few, including many socialists and welfarists, think that appropriate redistribution, by creating employment and raising incomes of the poor, can enhance growth. The evidence is unclear, but favours the first view and in some cases the third.

There is little evidence that growth *per se* can reduce relative poverty, inequality or social injustice beyond eliminating absolute destitution. During the 1980s the USA had rapid growth of both GDP and poverty (Dunkley, 1989) and today a quarter of all children under 12 (over 11 million) are hungry or close to hunger (Rich in *GW*, 7 April 1991:17). There is thus considerable reason to doubt the frequent assertion by expansionists, precautionists and the Pearce-WCED model that growth can help the environment by 'curing' poverty. In rich and poor countries alike poverty has been successfully combatted primarily through income and wealth redistribution, targetted health and welfare programmes, local employment generation and so forth, without much damage to work or other economic incentives, even if growth is slightly reduced.[34] In sum, growth is no panacea for either poverty or the environment, so any slight reduction for redistributive purposes seems warranted if required.

As regards inter-generational equity (the distribution of resources between current and future generations), mainstream economic theory leaves it to the market to decide appropriate 'discount rates' (the rate used by firms to calculate returns on investment projects and resource development). The higher the discount rate selected the faster the depletion of resources, and, arguably, the more the rights of future generations are 'discounted'. Precautionist economists often accept a modicum of government intervention to lower the discount rate. Environmentalists, however, argue that discount rates are too high, that social costs are excluded from the calculations, that future generations cannot 'bid' for their share and that rates should be set close to nought. Socialists have had little to say on the matter and perhaps should take a stronger stance.

There are several rationales for the mainstream expansionist view that resource development be left to markets and not be restrained on behalf of future generations. One rationale is that there appears to be plenty of resources at least for the 'foreseeable' future, so we need not restrain ourselves (eg. Drake and

Nieuwenhuysen, 1988:22). But, as I argued above, this is not factually correct, and for many forecasters the 'foreseeable' future is very short. Another rationale holds that technology may render some resources redundant, so these will be wasted if we do not use them now. This argument is absurd because we cannot anticipate future redundancies and, contrariwise, future innovations may require resources we have decided to gobble up. A third rationale, echoed by West Indian economist Sir Arthur Lewis, a Fabian and normally a progressive sort of chap, questions why we should 'stay poor so that the life of the human race may ... be extended for a further century or so', and suggests we leave 'the distant centuries to look after themselves'.[35] I regard this position as morally unacceptable and suggest that we should aim at very long-term survival, with the notion of bequest built into resource allocation decisions (see below).

The more usual mainstream rationale (eg. by Solow, 1974) is that we are obliged only to pass on knowledge and a high standard of living, irrespective of whether we transfer resources to future generations as materials *in* the ground or constructed capital *on* the ground (what I earlier termed the 'capital compensation' process). Some claim that our descendants will be richer for our innovative efforts so we should not worry about them too much.

I believe that these arguments are untenable for they erroneously imply that there is a smooth, complete transfer from mines to capital and that the latter is durable, whereas one estimate suggests that only six per cent of 'active materials' are embodied in durable goods, the remainder being 'converted into waste residuals as fast as it is extracted' (Ayers and Kneese, 1983:93). Nor is capital infinitely durable. The UK and US are now discovering, and Australia will soon find, that infrastructure deteriorates over a 50-100 year cycle, thus requiring maintenance and eventual replacement (Dunkley, 1989). Many buildings are only lasting a few decades, some computers barely five years and many consumer goods just a year or two. Our waste is astronomical and not all is recoverable. Future generations may appreciate the knowledge we bequeath them, but will also want some resources.

Pearce et al suggest that human-made capital can never fully compensate for the loss of natural capital (renewable and non-renewable resources) because the two forms of capital are not perfectly substitutable, future technological links between them are uncertain, degradation of natural capital may be irreversible and the poor suffer more from environmental damage than the rich. Pearce et al therefore advocate the concept of 'constant natural capital', which involves compensatory enhancement of renewable resources as non-renewable resources are depleted, so that the total value is kept constant irrespective of the value of human-made capital (Pearce et al, 1989; Barbier, 1989). A few countries have begun separate natural capital accounts for this purpose but I suspect that the prospects for constancy are problematic. I suggest that for optimum inter-generational equity we must seek to bequeath our heirs a reasonable share of resources, well maintained ecosystems, appropriately improved knowledge and certain other attributes of sustainability. If this entails lower discount rates and less immediate resource exploitation then slower growth will result, and this must be treated as a morally justified concomitant of inter-generational equity.

In conclusion, economic factors which tend to limit growth include diminishing returns to production inputs, the rising proportion of services and 'positional' goods, the costs of urbanisation, infrastructure depreciation and the need to ensure social and inter-generational equity. The effects of these factors may not be felt for many years yet and there may be a growth boom in the 1990s as some forecasters predict, but I consider it unlikely. Moreover, as I suggest below, a variety of social and demographic factors may limit growth even further and technology may not rescue it to the extent that many expansionists hope.

□ TECHNOLOGICAL LIMITS

As discussed already, a key argument of expansionists is that technology can 'de-couple' output from resource-energy inputs and from polluting side effects, so that eventually most forms of growth will be sustainable. During a tour of Australia in the 1970s the late Herman Kahn declared that humans can find solutions more quickly than they can create problems, a note of technological optimism which is largely a leap of faith. Certainly innovation will continue, but faith based merely on the probability of breakthroughs and an assumption of appropriateness seems at best unwise, at worst foolish. One critic of this view argues that economists do not allow sufficiently for uncertainty (Perrings, 1987:12 and 157). Solow (1974) admits to uncertainty but argues that the search for technological solutions is just as likely to succeed as to fail. This is true but unwise when dangers are high and erring on the side of caution is warranted.

More specifically, I suggest that there are five major problems with reliance on technological solutions. The first is that technology does not seem to be 'de-coupling' us from resources or pollution as rapidly as is generally thought, and improvements may be counteracted by further growth (see earlier in this chapter). Second, there is some evidence that there are now diminishing returns to technological innovation, and it has been suggested that industrialists are more aware of technological limitations than economists. The costs of research and product innovation are increasing faster than inflation, but most technological forecasts have been wildly over-estimated.[36] Software costs, organisational problems and innumerable hidden complexities are slowing the spread of electronic technologies, so that during the 1980s productivity improvements failed to show up in most sectors using high-tech innovations.[37] Computerised systems are also reducing competition in some sectors (Porter, 1990:36). If such trends continue there will be limits to the possibilities for growth through technology. The other three problems examined below particularly involve limits to the desirability of growth through technology.

The third problem is that many new technologies have the potential for adverse social impacts in a wide range of spheres such as privacy, computer crime, social patterns, sexual morays, literacy, culture, skills and employment. Such impacts are difficult to measure and disagreement about their implications is common. As regards the impact of micro-electronic technologies on employment, for example, early forecasts ranged from huge job gains to massive job losses. Neither extremes have eventuated, but perhaps partly because the diffusion of many technologies has not been as rapid as predicted. Although in theory technology can generate employment through what I call 'adjustment mechanisms' (eg. demand for new services or export generation) and 'adaptive mechanisms' (reduced working hours or more leisure), in practice the outcome is not certain. Many high-tech systems are proving to be more job-displacing and less recession-proof than expected, while demand for new services or leisure is sluggish (Forester, 1987). Such trends are causing 'jobless growth' in many sectors, which results in the need for a continuing 'treadmill' of growth in other sectors to generate new employment, and it is unclear how much longer this can continue. Post-industrial theorists such as Toffler suggest that it can continue indefinitely so long as we all accept the dictates of the 'information society' and computerise ourselves. But many are resisting these urgings in favour of a less risky and less growth-dependent model.

The fourth problem is that new technologies such as microelectronics are not as 'clean' as their protagonists claim, while some high technology systems have serious inherent dangers and even the potential for catastrophe. A remarkable study by US sociologist Charles Perrow found that the conjunction between human fallibilities, excessively complex technologies and the occasional failure of so-called 'fail-safe' systems renders accidents inevitable. The further conjunction between this fact and the catastrophic potential of some technologies makes them extremely undesirable and ecologically risky. Perrow therefore advocates the abolition of technologies such as nuclear power and the severe restriction of biotechnology, a proposal with which I fully concur.[38]

The final problem with technological solutions is that many technologies involve vicious circles of escalating problems and unknown impacts. A classic case is that of pesticides and related agro-chemicals. Effective at first, they have now created a host of adverse ecological effects and health problems, while their effectiveness has gradually been undermined by increasing pest resistance. Few strains of pests or weeds in the world are now wholly susceptible to chemicals and up to 30 species are resistant to all known pesticides. Comparable concerns apply to genetic engineering and other forms of biotechnology which are now creating novel biota whose likely ecological impacts are unknown. Such products include bacteria for leaching of minerals and for algal ocean harvesting, and an array of new agricultural species. The global corporate controllers of these technologies often poach Third World germplasm and create products which suit their businesses, such as plants which are resistant to pesticides rather than to pests! Some advocates of technology are really seeking further growth rather than environmental solutions *per se*, a notable case being those scientists who claim that future replacement of natural products by biotechnology will enable us to cut more forests now.[39]

Some products of the latest scientific revolutions will doubtless prove useful but, as noted above, the benefits are usually over-rated, the costs are under-estimated and the dangers are increasing. Another set of technologies being proposed, 'nanotechnologies' or the building of new life forms from the molecular level, entail so many dangers that one social scientist has already advocated that they should not be allowed to come to fruition (Milbrath, 1989:246). In many cases simpler, safer solutions are available. With pests, for instance, there is strong evidence that much infestation is due to modern agricultural methods such as monocropping and non-rotation, so that partly-traditional organic alternatives would be preferable and appear viable.[40] The search for new technologies will continue but should be controlled through participatory democratic structures.

The relentless technological quest is largely due to our concept of progress, which I call 'linear technological determinism' because it is perceived in terms of rising complexity and it rejects simple, traditional options. Conservator biologist Paul Ehrlich says that it is economists rather than scientists who believe in technological panaceas, and this is instanced by computer pioneer, Joseph Weizenbaum, who now rejects excessive use of computers because he believes that they prevent us 'pursuing what is truly valuable'.[41] There are severe limits to what technology can do. It can do little, for instance, to solve our most urgent conservation problem, that of declining species diversity (Conway in Wilson, 1988). In sum, many new and forthcoming technologies may make further growth possible, but may be of questionable benefit and might render such growth undesirable in many respects.

□ POPULATION LIMITS

The population issue entered social science debates in 1798 when Malthus first suggested that growth of human numbers outstrips food supply (others later said all production), thus requiring periodic misery and rises in the death rate to control them. Less dismal scientists eventually discovered that technology could 'postpone', if not repeal, the Law of Diminishing Returns, that human ingenuity could adjust output to population (the inverse of Malthus) and that, as a bonus, population could be self-limiting when mortgages became universal and children were no longer cost effective. Thereafter economists could, in clear conscience, cheerfully recommend that productive capacity expand indefinitely to meet the rising expectations of a decelerating population.

Some conservators, often tagged as 'neo-Malthusians', are less confident, believing that Malthus' prognosis was right but premature. They see the current global tally of 5.36 b people as a major cause of most resource and environmental problems, so that projections of 6 b in 2000, 8.5 b in 2025 and 12 b or more in 2100 (WCED, 1990:Ch.4) are unlikely to be sustainable. A few think that world population is already greatly excessive and want something more like 500 m (eg. Naess, 1989:149), to be achieved, of course, through attrition and less-than-replacement birth rates. Actually, most industrial countries have more or less achieved this now and will attain zero population growth (ZPG) within a decade or two, but will nevertheless add 230 m to the world's population by 2025 (WCED, 1990:144).

Despite some progress, however two major problems remain. The first is that population growth rates are high in those Third World countries least able to handle the impact, and control programmes get mixed results. The solutions most touted by Western 'experts' are accelerated industrialisation, urbanisation and the mortgage revolution. But many governments and non-government agencies are now having more success with 'grass roots' strategies such as village-based development, community-level security, appropriate education, better health care, contraceptive information, employment and 'empowerment' for women.[42]

The second problem is that rising per capita consumption can counteract lower population growth. Rich countries use over 80 per cent of the world's resources, the USA alone taking 40 per cent, Japan uses over 50 per cent of all tropical timber and many industrial countries import more than five times the volume of resources that they generate at home. Just 17 m Australians use as many resources as 1,000 m Africans (Beale and Fray, 1990:164).

The average US dog consumes as much as the average Indian and the average US human 137 times as much (Pereira and Seabrook, 1990:84). Demand by rich countries is therefore probably indirectly responsible for more ecological destruction than Third World peasants, and it is highly unlikely that the Earth could support a much larger population at even current US profligate living standards (Durning in Brown, 1991; Agarwal, 1987:178 ff).

Australia currently has the second highest population growth rate in the OECD after Turkey (1.7 per cent per annum) at which rate we will reach 30 m in 2021 and 60 m by 2070 (*Age*, 12 July 1990). Immigration accounts for about half the present growth. Many environmentalists think this high growth rate puts unsustainable pressure on our already damaged ecosystems and one scientist, Tim Flannery, thinks the optimum would be 12 million, five million fewer than now (*Sunday Age*, 7 April 1991). Some commentators, along with 65 per cent of Australians (Poll, *Age*, 29 May 1990) want immigration reduced and the $1.9 b annually spent on migrant assistance gradually shifted to conservation. I broadly agree with this so long as it phased in gradually and we continue with some refugee and reunion immigration. In sum, rapid growth rates of population and per capita consumption are straining the Earth and further economic growth possibilities are thereby limited. This situation is probably not sustainable and so growth rates of both will have to be reduced in the near future. As Mahatma Gandhi once said, there is enough for everyone's need, but not for some people's greed (Shiva, 1989:6).

☐ SOCIAL LIMITS

Although this category will be treated briefly, it is in some ways the most complex and perhaps the most important category of limits. The nature of socio-political systems is ultimately determined by the attitudes, norms and values of their populace, these being shaped by religion, culture and a variety of traditions, but now also by elite opinion via media in a 'mass society'. There is evidence that in earlier times people and societies, especially in the East, held values which incorporated the ideal of harmony between people and Nature, which does not mean, of course, that they accepted extreme poverty. Since the so-called Enlightenment the West has become dominated by values and ideas such as a belief in the necessity for continual 'progress', linear technological determinism (see above), scientism (the dominance of scientific thinking), economism (priority to economic concerns), a philosophy based on mechanistic models, the ascendancy of people over Nature and concepts of welfare based on purely materialistic considerations.

Today there are clear signs that the social outcomes of such values and concepts are often undesirable, many are inappropriate and most are being rejected by increasing numbers of people, who are wanting greater priority given to the environment and to non-material values. In the US and elsewhere, polls since the mid-1970s have found large majorities (up to 80 per cent on some issues) claiming to prefer more basic lifestyles, non-materialistic values, smaller systems, more harmony with Nature and so forth. A Norwegian poll of the mid-1970s found 76 per cent of respondents believing that their standard of living was *too high*, with similar majorities preferring a simpler life and being prepared to sacrifice high incomes if this would reduce stress.[43] Expression of such views may lack sincerity at this stage, but people also lack opportunities to practice such new-found values, so that full manifestation may take time. However, a major change in values is probably under way.

Sociologists, psychologists and economists have observed assorted discontents with affluence, and people in Western countries appear to be experiencing little increase in satisfaction as consumption rises. For instance, 'happiness' in US polls peaked in 1957. Other problems include rising crime, family breakdown, drug cults, increasing suicide rates and various other manifestations of 'alienation' from our mass-based, excessively complex, de-communalised society. Daniel Bell has suggested that industrial capitalism fosters values of consumerism and leisure on the demand side which undermine its work ethic on the supply side, thus rendering it socially unsustainable. It has also been observed that, rather than increasing leisure, the urbanised, computerised society has actually reduced it (by 37 per cent since 1973 for the average US citizen, for instance), while the plethora of modern household appliances appears to have had no impact on the time required for housework. Solutions proposed include

— 'small is beautiful' (smaller structures), 'slow is beautiful' (more natural time-based systems), 'human scale' (systems which all humans can manage), 'bioregionalism' (natural regions rather than nations), revival of 'community' concepts, a new age of religion and many more.[44]

An oft-mentioned but seldom acted-upon feature of our current global growth pattern is the gradual homogenisation of cultures, which is affecting almost all societies today and threatening destruction of some. The nature of the threat is not uniform, but its 'leading edge' is Westernisation in general and Americanisation in particular. As I am endeavouring to document elsewhere, even Australian language and culture is under more threat from Americanisation than people realise. A wide range of US icons, images and what I call the 'hi guys' idiom, which cannot be found in Australian traditions, is swamping us, particularly via TV channels obsessed with minimising costs to stay solvent. At the extreme end of this tragic spectrum are the many Third World societies now facing physical extinction, due in many cases to insatiable Western demand for timber or hamburgers. The human and cultural cost of all this, which is grossly under-estimated, makes the machine-chemical growth model in many ways undesirable and may in time force modification of its pace or direction. The critical social underlays of culture and tradition are largely ignored, sometimes even scorned, by Western development economists anxious to foster 'modernity'.

Finally, the question of where society is heading and whether that direction is appropriate or sustainable. Amongst the many conjectures it is useful to identify three streams. The first is the mainstream neo-classical economic and sociological view which projects continuation of the present high energy, rapid growth, machine-chemical model to a very high level of income and service-based affluence. The second, more left-leaning, view (often called 'post-Fordism'), projects and urges the democratisation of modern technology for enhanced egalitarian skills and for more participatory enterprises. Protagonists of this view hold that high material living standards can be retained, along with a 'clean' environment, through new high-tech methods of 'flexible specialisation' and 'human centred' technology, but only if technologies are democratically selected so as to avoid the old socially insensitive 'Fordist' systems. French neo-Marxist Andre

Gorz advocates a guaranteed minimum income, funded by taxes in high-tech productivity, so as to break the nexus between work and income and to liberate individuals from industrial routine.

The third stream (often called 'post-industrialism') projects and advocates a new form of environment-friendly 'qualitative' growth, with an economy based increasingly on services, information, computerised automation, flexible working arrangement and responsive social structures. The second two streams have recently produced valuable critiques of neo-classical economic tenets such as market allocation, rational calculation, consumer sovereignty and so on. The first stream is rather deterministic, whereas the others claim that their visions are alternative tendencies which should be fostered. The first stream neglects environmental, resource and equity issues, and so I oppose it. I sympathise with some strategies of the latter two streams, but I consider that they rely too heavily on decisions by profit-oriented firms, they may render us excessively dependent on high technologies, they under-estimate environmental concerns and they neglect culture and tradition by proposing merely an alternative form of modernity. All three streams overlook the fact that the so-called 'information society', which they all espouse to some degree, would require a continuing resource base and could not solve some of the more complex ecological problems discussed above.[45]

A fundamental issue underlying this debate is what constitutes human needs and how they should be satisfied. As noted earlier, mainstream theory tends to blend needs and wants, thenceforth insisting that humans are acquisitive animals whose wants cannot be satiated, a state which is absolute rather than socially conditioned (Thurow, 1981:120). Socialists are more inclined to see some wants as artificially created and capitalism as emphasising material and individual wants rather than collective and non-material needs. Both streams, however, tend to see needs as hierarchical, as being relative to social status and as being subject to the 'demonstration effect' (those 'with' are envied by those 'without'), so that needs are best met through growth until reasonably satiated, though the various streams differ on the type of economic system required.[46]

A new view amongst some environmentalists and alternative economic schools is that wants are 'socially constructed', while needs are finite, few, uniform across cultures and readily satisfiable. Basic needs consist of: — subsistence, protection, affection, understanding, participation, leisure, creativity, identity and freedom, each incorporating economic and non-economic, private and collective elements. Each culture decides differently whether and how to satisfy these needs, but any society can be more sustainable by minimising superfluous artificial wants and by better satisfying basic needs.

This view implies, as I see it, a very different concept of human nature from that of the mainstream, seeing people in a Gandhian light — as need-oriented rather than greed-oriented; satisficing more than optimising; wanting security more than income; partly altruistic rather than wholly individualistic; wanting a mix of collective provision and personal responsibility; substantially moral rather than largely calculating; spiritual as much as material; living for the past and future as much as the present; and protective rather than exploitative of Nature. This is a much more positive view of people than is found in mainstream theory, especially in neo-classical economics, and is consistent with current research results.[47] Such a view of human nature would help explain why there is growing dissatisfaction with material consumption, concern about environmental damage and cultural homogenisation, boredom with the television society and so forth. But this view also explains how conservative political interests can sometimes induce in people fear of economic insecurity, preoccupation with income, predominantly short-term economic concerns, anti-government paranoia and convictions that growth is the solution.

In conclusion, of the factors discussed in the foregoing Sub-sections many (such as global warming) will in time place physical limits on future growth possibilities, while some factors appear to be already reducing production levels, notably land degradation and acid rain. Other factors, such as minor forms of pollution, might not be preventing physical sustainability for the foreseeable future, but are gradually inflicting ecological damage whose eventual impacts cannot be known as yet. Other factors again, such as social, cultural or aesthetic impacts and perhaps even destruction of some wilderness areas and wild animals, may be physically and ecologically sustainable, but are extremely undersirable for the maintenance of a rich, diverse human and non-human life on Earth.

The pattern and extent of such constraints will be difficult to predict. It may eventuate, for instance, that value changes, economic limitations or adverse social reaction to the undesirable aspects of growth may bring it to an end well before physical limits come into play. My conclusion, however, is that many sub-systems of the machine-chemical model are unsustainable in a variety of respects, and that the economy will not be able to 'marry' the environment until the unsustainable sub-systems are organised in ways which are much more acceptable to the would-be bride. The next sub-section will examine whether or not the Pearce-WCED model and other comparable proposals for SD are any more sustainable.

• ANYONE FOR GROWTH?

When, in his 1985 Second Inaugural Address, former US President Ronald Reagan proclaimed that there are no limits to growth (Milbrath, 1989:126) he doubtless had not been warned of Boulding's quip that only lunatics and economists believe in perpetual growth. Surveys have shown that US business leaders are the only professional group to agree with Reagan, even their British and German equivalents harbouring some doubts (Milbrath, 1989:126-7). In recent years, however, such groups have had their faith in growth resuscitated by the WCED and its Canadian secretary general, Jim MacNeill (1990), who are urging a 'new era of growth' based on the allegedly more sustainable Pearce-WCED model (my term).

Details of this model remain sketchy but in principle it would differ from the machine-chemical model in some important and fundamental ways. In my summation, the WCED's approach begins from five key propositions: — i. basic human needs are not currently being adequately met, particularly in the poorer countries; ii. current technologies and social organisation limit the capacity of the environment to meet present and future needs (because of ecological damage); iii. the world is faced with a series of inter-linked crises (poverty, environmental decline, economic instability, debt, social problems), perhaps the most serious being that in many countries poverty is forcing people into inadvertant environmental destruction (eg. cutting the few remaining trees for firewood); iv. future development must be compatible with social and inter-generational equity; v. renewed growth must be part of the solution, but it will need to be qualitatively different from that of the past.

From these propositions the WCED derives a number of more specific proposals for changes to the way we organise our economic, political and economic systems, including technological and administrative re-organisations, mechanisms for improving the environment and enhancing the natural resource base, de-centralisation of political power and urban structures, RETP de-coupling (my term), the merging of economic and environmental considerations in decision-making, new international economic arrangements which will strengthen the position of poor countries and other vaguely defined systemic improvements aimed at democratisation (WCED, 1990:esp. p.109).

To this Pearce et al (1989) have added detailed proposals regarding environmental improvement (mainly via taxes), resource accounting procedures, systems for valuing environmental assets and the concept of 'constant natural capital'. I use the term 'Pearce-WCED model' because the respective approaches of Pearce et al and the WCED are of a similar spirit, and are complementary in their areas of speciality. Both draw the crucial inference of a direct relationship between growth and environmental quality (PW in Box 3) and both therefore recommend continued or even accelerated growth. In particular, MacNeill (1990) and the WCED (1990) claim that to eliminate world poverty, to provide for a growing population and to alleviate environmental pressures, a five to ten-fold rise in global GDP will be required before growth can safely level off. This is estimated to entail global annual per capita growth rates of 3.2 to 4.7 per cent for the next fifty years, with annual GDP growth rates of 5 per cent in Asia, 5.5 per cent in Latin America and 6 per cent in Africa (MacNeill, 1990:111-2).

I have grave reservations about the viability of the Pearce-WCED model. First, it relies heavily on market mechanisms and RETP de-coupling, the efficacy of which I have questioned earlier in this chapter and will further criticise later in the book. Second, although it says the 'right' things about environmental problems, poverty, global inequity and the need for world-wide institutional reform, its operational proposals are vague, its grasp of the political implications is tenuous and it is unclear how the transition from unsustainable systems to a sustainable model would be made in practice. Third, it greatly under-estimates the enormity of the institutional change required, particularly in industrialised countries.

Fourth, the Pearce-WCED model's crucial assumption that poverty causes environmental deterioration is over-simplified and dubious. There are indeed links, but causality may be equally or more in the other direction. Third World poverty is a complex outcome of factors such as colonial exploitation; excessive industrialisation relative to agricultural capacity; over-exploitation of resources by commercial interests, often to meet the demands of rich countries or wealthy local elites; importation of inappropriate technologies and development models via self-interested 'tied' aid from rich countries; excessively rapid population growth relative to fragile resource bases; and the breakdown of traditional socio-economic and cultural systems under Western-induced pressure for development. In many traditional societies people lived sustainably on forest resources and varied, locally-supplied diets, whereas 'development' has forced many into imported diets and unsustainable farming practices.

Given such complex causes Western-style growth models have proved much less suitable than a variety of newly-emerging approaches which include: — more appropriate labour-intensive technologies; locally-based self-help programmes; more participatory, democratic administrative structures; co-operative management of resources; 'empowerment' of women and the poor; and restoration of traditional agricultural systems based on conservation. I call this a 'green villages' approach, a term currently being used in India. The WCED seems to be aware of this approach but accords it little weight in proposed solutions. I believe, however, that general adoption of a 'green villages' approach by governments and development agencies would be much better environmentally, economically, socially and culturally than the growth-oriented gamble advocated by the WCED and expansionists everywhere.[48]

Fifth, for reasons already discussed above in other contexts, I am sceptical about the WCED's supposition that a 'new era of growth' could relieve poverty, reduce population growth and reduce pressures on the environment by getting people out of forests and into cities. MacNeill (1990:114) proposes renewed growth as the first step to SD, and the WCED (1990:16) describes its proposed qualitative shift to a sustainable model as needing to be 'powered by a continuing flow of wealth from industry'. Yet neither have considered the fact that such growth, starting from a base in the existing machine-chemical model, may do more damage than it will ever cure through the above-mentioned mechanisms. Furthermore, the growth targets sought (see above) are, in my opinion, completely unfeasible because they are about the same rates as most countries averaged during the last two decades or so, and experience suggests that peak growth rates are seldom maintained for more than a decade. Such targets also ignore the variety of possible limits to growth which I have discussed above. I argue, therefore, that the Pearce-WCED model may not ultimately differ much in its impact from the machine-chemical model and I will presently propose an alternative approach.

In previous sub-sections I argued that long-term growth may be both unfeasible and undesirable. However, some expansionists, particularly in the US, argue that high growth must be maintained in order to strengthen defence and national power. I counter-argue that legitimate defence needs should be sought through collective security (see Milbrath, 1989:Ch.15) and that the concept of national power should be rejected. Many also argue that continued growth is necessary for a country to be internationally competitive, but much evidence now suggests that it is innovation which brings competitiveness and growth, not the reverse (see Porter, 1990). Even the great improvements in health and longevity which have been widely attributed to growth now appear in jeopardy from the environmental crisis, and these would not necessarily be sacrificed by alternative less growth-oriented development models.

Virtually all expansionists and precautionists, including Pearce et al and the WCED, insist that growth is required to generate more resources for research and development (R and D), including for environmental purposes. I disagree because, even with decreased macro growth, resources for environmentally-related R and D could be obtained by raising the total R and D share of GDP, by shifting resources from defence, consumer goods, cosmetics and other areas of questionable social value, or by a more efficient allocation of research resources, particularly in the energy sector where the current allocation is heavily weighted against 'soft' alternatives. Australia's R and D picture is better than is generally thought as our non-military research, at 0.7 per cent of GDP, is above the OECD average of 0.55 per cent, our higher education sector and ratio of research personnel are well above OECD averages and other indicators are around the norm for our type of economy.[49] A switch of R and D resources to the environment would, therefore, not necessarily be as damaging to other sectors as is often claimed.

At the other end of the spectrum some conservators, notably Ehrlich and Suzuki, have advocated negative economic growth (NEG), to the horror of mainstream economists and politicians who say that such a policy would bring massive unemployment and poverty as it did in recent recessions. Advocates of NEG want it phased in gradually, of course, but it nevertheless should be treated with caution because it is unclear by how much we would have to 'un-grow' to solve target problems, and resultant social disruption may bring all environmental policies into disrepute amongst some people. The main purpose of NEG is to cut RETP, but because growth occurs at the margin a long period of ZEG or NEG would be required to significantly reduce total RETP, and even then environmental improvement is not guaranteed unless appropriate structural changes also occur. I propose that growth should not be a target *per se*, but should be determined as a residual outcome once all sustainability requirements have been fulfilled, which may entail some NEG in the long-term.

In conclusion, I have argued in this chapter that we are in the midst of an environmental crisis caused by a complex mix of unsustainable systems, over-population, excessive per capita consumption and the high-RETP nature of the machine-chemical economy. The result is severe limits on the possibility and desirability of long-term growth. While the machine-chemical model clearly involves a trade-off between income (or GDP) levels and environmental standards (the MC curve in Box 3), the Pearce-WCED model claims an ability to 'marry' income growth and the environment by using a qualitatively different approach to growth in which the two variables are complementary (PW in Box 3). I have expressed doubts as to whether the latter model would be greatly different from the former in its environmental effects, especially as it seeks accelerated long-term growth. I suspect that its shape would be more like a reverse S ($P_1 W_1$ in Box 3), eventually involving return to a trade-off.

In the next two chapters I will examine alternative solutions and propose what I call a 'green-red' model whose course would facilitate some growth but would probably have a lower income ceiling in the longer-term than the other models (the GR curve in Box 3). Given limits to growth, the future of growth and the fate of the environment are extremely uncertain and a high-growth policy seems as irrational as a driver accelerating whilst debating with his or her passengers how close they are to the edge of a cliff. I accept the concept of sustainability but prefer to avoid the word 'development' because of its regrettable association with growth. My definition of sustainability (No. 9 in Box 2) is based on the notion that we must organise our economic, political, social and cultural systems and sub-systems for sustainability, a notion hinted at by the WCED. This would require us to seek 'ecologically and socially sustainable organisation of systems' (ECSSOS), as I will further explain later in the book.

5 COLOUR-CODED SOLUTIONS

THIS chapter looks more closely at various theoretical approaches to environmental problems and solutions, which are often flippantly colour-coded for convenience. I argue that a mix of 'green' and 'red' concepts provides the most suitable basis for sustainable socio-economic systems.

• 'BLUE' — JUST GIVE ME A MARKET

This school of thought is based on neo-classical theory which suggests that all resource allocation is best done through markets. Most 'blues' adopt what I call the 'externalities' aproach to environmental problems, which holds that resources, such as clean air or unpolluted water, are under-priced 'goods' and are therefore misallocated. The market fails to recognise the cost of unclean air and so produces more of it than is required, this excess being known as an 'externality' or 'external diseconomy'. The main solution advocated is to rectify the market failure by 'internalising' the externalities, primarily through an appropriate tax on the unwanted output (ie. pollutants, etc.). Several other approaches are used, notably the 'commons' approach which sees air, water, trees and so forth

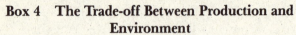

Box 4 The Trade-off Between Production and Environment

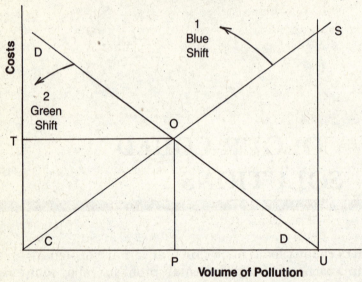

- The DD curve is the cost of abating pollution (or other environmental damage) in terms of money or foregone production. In a sense it represents the 'demand' for pollution as it is the amount of output demanded for a given volume of pollution.
- The SC curve embodies the environmental and other social costs of production, thus representing the 'supply' of pollution or other environmental damage.
- Without penalties or other costs for causing pollution firms and consumers will 'demand' (or at least inadvertently cause) as much pollution as possible — U the 'unpriced' level of pollution.
- 'Blue' economists see point O as an 'optimal' trade-off between production requirements and the social costs of production, resulting in an optimum level of pollution — P. This level must, however, be enforced by taxes or penalties — T. A higher level of taxes would reduce P further but would not be 'optimal' as consumers may whinge about the costs.

> - 'Blue' economists also advocate technologies and other
>   innovations to reduce the social costs of production,
>   which can be illustrated here as a shift of the SC curve
>   (Arrow 1) so as to lower P. Greens do not disagree with
>   this, but believe that a reduction in demand for
>   production, or even elimination of some demands
>   (Arrow 2), may also be required, in order to dramatically
>   reduce P.

as 'common property' resources and subject to competitive over-
exploitation. For this problem 'blues' propose that individual
property rights be attached to all resources so that 'responsible'
private ownership will encourage efficiency and prevent
externalities.

'Blue' solutions begin from the notion that there is a trade-
off between all virtues and vices of life, in this case the trade-
off being between consumer goods and resultant social 'bads'
(pollution, traffic congestion, accidents) as in the diagram (Box
4). The 'optimum' trade-off (O) results in an optimum or 'socially
efficient' level of pollution (P), below which there would be 'not
enough' pollution because abatement entails costs (in money or
foregone goods) which are higher than the public wishes to pay.
This concept is galling to environmentalists but it has a pragmatic
logic. The main problem is that social costs (SC) are difficult
to measure, especially in the case of long-term effects, and so the
optimum (O) is indeterminate, whereas abatement costs (DD) are
usually easily valued in money terms. So normal market
operations will not consider social costs (SC) at all and will
produce as much pollution as necessary (U in Box 4).

'Blue' economists have therefore devised a five-step approach
to dealing with environmental problems. The first step is to place
monetary values on environmental assets which have not hitherto
been thought amenable to valuation. This has resulted in several
new concepts of value, these being — i. commodity value (assets
which have a market and can be monetised, eg. useful plants
or animals); ii. amenity value (an environmental asset desired for
itself and perhaps partly monetised — eg. a national park); iii.
option value (option to use i or ii in future rather than now);
iv. existence value (desired but not used or monetised — eg. remote

wilderness or species diversity); v. bequest value (resources set aside for future generations). The non-monetary values are then measured through 'surrogate markets' by one of three methods — a. hedonic pricing (comparison of asset prices where environment is a variable — eg. values of similar houses where one is in a polluted locality); b. travel cost technique (use of travel costs to assess people's valuation of an asset — eg. national parks or recreation areas); c. contingent valuation (surveys of people's 'willingness to pay' to save an asset).

The second step is to use such valuations for specifying the social cost curve (SC), the optimal trade-off point (O) and the 'optimum' pollution level (P). The third step is to place an appropriate cost on polluting activities so as to charge polluters at T (in Box 4), thus lowering actual pollution levels from U to P. For this purpose there are two wide-ranging methods. The first consists of regulations, controls or licencing so as to enforce emission standards (at P in Box 3) with fines and other such penalties. The second consists of what could broadly be called 'pollution taxes', or what New Right 'blues' like to call 'incentives', of which there are six major categories — a. charges (*pro rata* tax penalties, at T in Box 3, on all pollution above P); b. deposit-refund systems (mainly to encourage recycling); c. market creation (encouraging markets for recycled products and emissions 'trading' between polluters); d. enforcement fees (fines, bonds, etc.); e. subsidies (loans, research assistance, tax concessions for anti-pollution expenditures, etc.); f. removal of tax or other assistance which damages the environment (see OECD, 1989).

The fourth step is to supplement these micro-level actions with better macro-level national accounting, for which two types of amendments are proposed — a. separate natural resource accounts so as to track depletion of minerals, forests and so on; b. adjustment of GDP to exclude 'bads' (eg. car accidents or pollution clean-ups) and 'defensive expenditures' (eg. costs of environmental protection, occupational safety, law and order and urban restoration). A fifth step, advocated mainly by the more zealous 'deep blues', is to better clarify existing property rights and to create appropriate new private property rights (see above).

With this approach most 'blues' believe the worst externalities can be internalised (i.e. pollutants optimally abated) and new environment-enhancing technologies can be encouraged, thus shifting SC to a less polluting position (Arrow 1 in Box 4). They think all this can be done without sacrificing our current standards of living or material output (no shift in DD — Box 4). Recent years have seen the emergence of 'light blues', who have been very active in devising the above-mentioned valuation and accounting systems. They hold that environmental impacts (P in Box 4) should be set at tolerance levels which are within the Earth's ecological capacity to renew resources and absorb wastes, even if this means small sacrifices of consumption (Arrow 2, Box 4). 'Light blues' believe that by and large the above five-step policy approach can be effective, although they are willing to accept a higher level of government intervention than 'deeper blues'.[50]

Needless to say, however, there are some problems with these 'blue' solutions. Valuation (step 1) remains partly subjective, is imprecise, is usually incompletely specified, lacks standardised procedures and usually entails biases towards values measured quantitatively. Contingent valuation surveys show most promise and have demonstrated the public to be (theoretically) willing to pay for a wide range of environmental restoration. But the results can vary between regions, can be affected by income distribution and would be meaningless in a Third World non-monetary economy. Many conservationists contend that a price cannot be placed on beauty, ecological survival or other such 'assets' of intrinsic value. Valuations will always be disputed, as has happened with the 1990 RAC survey of opinion regarding Coronation Hill in Northern Australia. Extrapolation from a sample of 2,500 Australians suggested that people were apparently willing to pay A$647 m to save the site from mining, a stark contrast with the mere $80 m in likely export revenue. The business community has ridiculed the results as grossly over-pricing the environment, and has questioned the validity of the method. Despite its faults, however, valuation should be used for guidance in particular cases, but the valuation process will never completely substitute for discretionary decisions by government.

Establishing the optimum trade-off (step 2) can only be as accurate as the identification and valuation of social costs, but valuation is problematic, as argued above, and even some economists concede that many social costs will never be accounted for (Archibugi and Nijkamp, 1989:42). The 'optimum' (O in

Box 4) is usually arrived at through cost-benefit analysis (CBA), but this can be subjective, may be biased towards quantified values and will greatly under-estimate extreme, uncertain or irreversible social costs — eg. toxic chemicals or destruction of species (see Pearce in *Kyklos*, 29, 1979). Furthermore, the very concept of an optimum means that there will be residual emissions with some continuing long-term damage, and expansionists reject as impossible the complete elimination of pollution (eg. *Economist*, 1990:6). We cannot yet know what ecological effects long-term residual emissions will have, and thus the whole concept of 'optimum' or 'socially efficient' pollution should be treated with scepticism. In general 'blues' think that the optimum can be determined by the market, but, as I argued earlier, the market can be shown to be an unreliable, even if useful, instrument. Low-income and low-wealth humans get few 'money votes' in the market, while future generations, non-human species and ecosystems get none. Yet it can well be argued that these are constituencies which deserve a vote.

Enforcing the 'optimum' (step 3) is equally problematic. To date pollution standards and regulations have been the most common method used, but with only partial success in abating pollution. EPAs are highly vulnerable to under-funding and under-staffing, as in Australia at present, and to political emasculation, as in the US under Reagan. Economists claim that, relative to regulations, pollution taxes (see above) are more efficient and more effective, can encourage technological innovations and will better preserve competition, so they advocate a shift from regulation to taxes and other market-based incentives. But the 150 or so measures of this sort used in OECD countries to date have had limited success, as they have been set at unduly low levels due to corporate opposition or to enforcement difficulties. Some water charges and deposit systems have been successful, but in practice a mix of regulations and charges has been the norm, a situation which seems likely to continue (OECD, 1989; Common in ANU, 1990). A critical, but often overlooked, condition for successful pollution taxes is that demand for the taxed polluting products must be relatively 'elastic' (responsive), in which case little or no revenue will be raised by the tax. If demand is 'inelastic' (unresponsive), revenue can be raised but demand may not be greatly reduced. Some economists believe that demand is becoming less elastic in Western countries as people become innured to chronic inflation and volatile prices. If so, this would make market methods of pollution control less practicable than hitherto. Singapore, perhaps the first society to try reducing its car population, has found taxes ineffective and so is now imposing quotas (Wallace in *Sunday Age*, 18 August 1991). Furthermore, pollution taxes need monitoring even if less so than regulations, must be tailored to identified pollutants (there are tens of thousands of these), can favour large firms with big research budgets, or firms with other forms of market power, and may be repealed by pro-business governments. The tradeable emission permit system, favoured by many economists as a compromise between regulation and market-based incentives, can be efficient in theory because firms with the lowest abatement costs will buy the permits. In practice, however, tradeable permits may not be efficient under monopoly conditions, they can be complicated to monitor, they may redistribute emissions unpredictably and in principle they enshrine the 'right to pollute'. In reality extensive regulation will probably always be required, though governments should avoid ecologically damaging subsidies (eg. to nuclear power, to unsustainable agriculture and so forth).

Regarding the fourth step, adjustment of national accounts, some countries have already established natural resource accounts (eg. Norway, France and Indonesia) or alternative GDP measures (eg. Japan, US) and the latter have produced some interesting results. The Japanese Government's alternative 'net national welfare' (NNW) measure was higher than GNP before the 'economic miracle' of the 1960s but was outstripped by the latter as the growth 'miracle' boosted pollution from 0.2 to 13.8 per cent of NNW by 1970. Similar privately-designed measures in the US, such as that of Daly and Cobb, found that adjusted per capita welfare peaked around 1968, stayed constant in the 1970s and has declined ever since (Daly and Cobb, 1989; Brown in Brown, 1991). Most environmentalists support such alternative accounting systems, arguing that our current practices are akin to a company living off its capital rather than its income, a practice which is obviously unsustainable in the long-term. Despite their value as indicators, however, adjusted accounts can be readily ignored by government, and a current UN review has recommended against any form of GDP adjustment for environment or natural resources.[51] Adjusted accounts provide a guide to, not a substitute for, discretionary government action. In my view, however, such adjustments should be made and the amended indicators should be used as much as possible, although incomes would have to be fixed to an index based on marketed production so as to avoid inflation.

Finally, step five, the enhancement of private property rights, may have some applicability, particularly in former CPS countries, but is likely to prove an extremely limited solution. Private property rights are impractical where environmental assets are diffuse or indivisible, as so many are (eg. air, water and genetic diversity), or where there are multiple causes of a problem (eg. global warming or acid rain). More importantly, it has been shown in theory that even a profit maximising private owner will deplete a resource to extinction if the re-growth rate is lower than current rates of return, thereafter moving on to another area. This was borne out in practice when resource privatisation in the US last century, and under Reagan in the 1980s, raised exploitation rates above those required for sustainability. In a recent notorious US case a small firm which had sustainably harvested redwoods for several generations was taken over by large junk bond-financed asset-strippers, who promptly clear-felled the area to pay off their debts.[52] The notion proposed by some 'deep blues' that, given extended property rights, conservationists could buy the environments they wish to protect or restore, smacks of cuckoo land (see Porter in *Australian*, 18 September 1981). Some green zealots, including myself, are already doing this, but not all environmentally concerned people are willing or able to do so. The idea that the Earth should only survive if enthusiasts are rich enough to save it would be laughable if it were not so dangerous. Only a miniscule dent in the problem is possible in this way when the entire biosphere is at risk and when some damage may be irreversible, or may be curable only in the very long-term. The free enterprise market system is probably much more inefficient than property rights theorists assume (Smith in ANU, 1990:135), and alternatives are available, including some succussful Third World experiments in communal management of resources.[53]

In conclusion, it is clear that 'blue' models based on market processes, incentives, technological innovations and so forth can provide partial solutions at best and cannot adequately handle the complex skein of linked ecological problems we face today and in future, though elements of such models have some role to play. A disconcerting number of mainstream neo-classical economists confess to the fallibility of markets (eg. Arrow in Daly and Umana, 1981), or sufficiently so to question whether we should rely too heavily on market-based methods. More generally, 'blue' strategies also assume the perpetuation, largely in its contemporary form, of the industrial capitalist system, a system which other schools of thought consider to be inequitable and socially unsustainable.

• 'RED' — NOTHING TO LOSE BUT YOUR SOCIAL COSTS

A number of schools of economic thought reject the neo-classical emphasis on the efficacy of markets in general and the 'externality' approach to environmental problems in particular. In both respects many of these schools take what could be called the 'power' approach, which sees economic decisions working through market power rather than through self-equilibrating markets, including the power to inflict environmental damage on economically, politically or socially disfranchised groups in the community. Perhaps the two most prominent 'light red' schools are the post-Keynesians and the institutionalists, whose environmentalist pioneers include K. William Kapp, E. J. Mishan and Kenneth Boulding. As regards proposed solutions to environmental problems, institutionalists have devised a range of sophisticated policy interventions, planning systems and improved cost-benefit analysis techniques, although a few have advocated some unnecessarily draconian economic and popula-tion controls. 'Light reds' see environmental, social, cultural and other such problems as 'social costs' rather than 'externalities', which must be removed by collective action rather than be 'optimally internalised' through markets.

Socialists also arguably take the 'power' approach to economics in general and to the environment in particular, although, as I pointed out in Chapter 3, the main schools of socialism have usually had a variety of higher priorities. Marx and Engels were aware of the pollution and despoilation associated with the Industrial Revolution, and in one perspicacious passage Marx anticipated the problem of soil erosion through poor farming techniques and the urge for short-term profits. But Marx's general thrust was that Nature must be responsibly managed for human purposes and that socialism will inherit a developed infrastructure from capitalism, thence proceeding to a less materialistic affluence under communism. Later socialists, especially in the first two streams noted in Chapter 3, largely followed suit. Most Marxists believe that all societies must have highly developed 'forces of production' before they can shift from capitalism to socialism, and thus they often advocate industrial growth and high technology under capitalism in order to hasten this transition. This deterministic sequence can be disputed, and in my view it is no longer feasible, given the limits to growth. CPS regimes, which formerly predominated in the Soviet Union and Eastern Europe, and still in China, have created major environmental problems in the name of rapid industrial growth, 'people's livelihood' and Marxian value theory, their version of which for a long time discounted 'unproductive' services and valued raw materials merely at extraction cost.

'Reds' have now developed more cohesive views on the environment, but have gradually divided into a precautionist (with a few expansionists) tendency, especially among those from the predominant first two streams (see Chapter 3), and a conservator tendency, especially among those from the second two streams. To the extent that both tendencies take the 'power' approach to environmental (and other) problems, they both want democratisation of power structures and a redistribution of market power away from those who perpetuate what they see as capitalist 'growth-mania'. However, there are important differences between them. In particular, precautionist 'reds' have often been scornful of the alleged middle class, politically naive naturism of 'greenies', who allegedly place too much blame on industrialism and not enough on capitalism. They want solutions to be more 'red' than 'green'. Conservator 'reds' are more likely to see problems with industrialism itself and want solutions to be at least as much 'green' as 'red'.

The precautionist tendency advocates improved living standards via growth, redistribution and technological innovation directed towards an equitable affluence in a creative, challenging society. Precautionist 'reds' believe that the capitalist growth 'treadmill' is unable to create equitable or rewarding social outcomes and thus it spawns consumerist sublimation, whereas socialism can bring more satisfaction with less growth and can solve environmental problems by building ecological factors into economic planning. But most precautionist 'reds' consider that continuing growth will be needed for some time yet to maintain improvements and create jobs. Labour and Social Democratic governments have generally pursued demand management policies with a pro-growth bias, adhering to Keynes' dictum that we must worship the god of avarice for a little longer (he thought a century or so) until riches are reasonably widely bestowed. Emerging 'post-Fordist' schools hold that extended citizen control over all political, technological and work processes, along with more flexible employment systems based on appropriate 'smart' technologies, can elicit less de-skilling, de-humanising and polluting social outcomes than currently prevail (eg. Mathews, 1989). The precautionist tendency also draws on the 'lighter red' schools such as institutionalists or post-Keynesians (above), and would probably accept some 'blue' solutions such as valuation or pollution taxes, though most faith is placed in interventionism and in striving for socialism.

The conservator tendency is inspired by the anarchist stream, from Kropotkin to US 'social ecologist' Murray Bookchin, and by a diverse romantic intellectual stream from the aesthete Ruskin, through Morris, an ideosyncratic Marxist, to Tawney, a Christian, a scholar and a prominent Fabian (Quotations 3 and 4, Box 1). The concerns of conservator 'reds' are as diverse as their backgrounds but they broadly focus on the social, aesthetic, environmental, cultural and even spiritual impacts of industrial capitalism. The socialist utopian ideas of William Morris have influenced the German Greens (Papadakis, 1984:54–5). Contemporary conservator 'reds' are close to 'greens' in some respects and often are active environmentalists. As such they provide a key link in what I shall describe below as the 'greening of the red'.[54] The main environmentalist criticisms of 'reds' are that they do not adequately understand ecological processes or the various limits to growth, an accusation which is not without foundation. On the other hand, however, activist 'reds' have developed a grasp of political and social subtleties and 'light red' political parties have a wealth of administrative experience, all of which 'greens' will require in greater measure if they wish to form political movements.

• 'LIGHT GREEN' — ALL THINGS BRIGHT AND BEAUTIFUL

The predominant view of most conservationist and environmentalist organisations could be described as 'light green'. Whilst many would to some extent accept the 'externalities', the 'commons' or even the 'power' approach to explaining environmental problems, I suggest that their framework is best described as an 'ethical' approach because they believe that solutions should be based on environmental and social ethics rather than on conventional economic logic. Few 'light greens' are centrally concerned about economic losses in the economy–environment trade-off process, fearing potential environmental losses to be more serious and grossly under-valued. Loss of a few species is far worse than loss of a few consumer goods. This is in contrast to environmentally sensitive 'light blue' economists such as David Pearce who are concerned to minimise such economic losses and to get the numbers right.

On a 'blue'–'red' spectrum ranging from unfettered markets to centralised planning 'light greens' occupy a wide middle ground. Amory Lovins and other 'energy optimists', as I call them, argue that appropriate technological innovation, free markets and abolition of government subsidies to 'hard' energy paths, such as nuclear power, are the key policies for both a 'cleaner' environment and higher living standards. Lester Brown and other members of the prestigious Worldwatch Institute in Washington (Brown, 1981) are primarily concerned with meeting basic needs without damaging ecosystems, so they support markets and capitalism to the extent that these are effective while accepting that some government intervention is necessary. Most 'light greens' acknowledge that there will be many technological solutions, while counselling against total reliance thereon. A few 'light greens' like Barry Commoner support 'red' solutions such as state intervention in technological decisions and comprehensive planning. Advocates of totalitarian solutions are few in number amongst 'light greens' and have received undue attention by critics of environmentalism.

Some 'light greens' are prepared to argue partly within a conventional framework and so accept the need for valuation, cost-benefit trade-off analysis, revised national accounting and even some extension of private property rights. The doyen of 'light green' economists is US scholar, Herman Daly, who writes in the most respected economic journals and currently advises the World Bank on environmental issues. Daly is highly critical of 'blues' reliance on markets, but advocates market-based interventionism through auctioned 'depletion quotas' (in effect, heavy taxes on resource use) and transferrable birth licences (for holding population to ZPG — originally Boulding's idea). He also favours strict limits on income differentials and private wealth-holding, but otherwise eschews radical socialism and thinks that property will remain predominantly private. His proposals have been dismissed by mainstream economists as impractically bureaucratic, destructive of incentives and possibly counter-productive (Tietenberg, 1988:498).

Daly bills his system as a 'steady state', a less dismal successor to the nineteenth century concept of a 'stationary state' in which poverty was seen as the main check on population explosion. Mill (Quotation 2, Box 1) was the first economist to welcome the stationary state on environmental and aesthetic grounds and to suggest that misery need not prevail. Daly defines his 'steady state' as nil growth in RETP and population, but continued qualitative growth in the finer things of life and various forms of non-material progress. He holds that conventional economics focuses only on the middle of the means-ends spectrum — ie. resource inputs and prosaic material outputs — thus over-blowing the virtues of GDP growth.

By and large 'light greens' concur with Daly's prescription, although some accept continued GDP growth where technology can 'de-couple' it from RETP and pollution, a notion which I criticised earlier as being unreliable. However, 'deeper greens' (next sub-section) regard their 'lighter' counterparts as anthropocentric (human-centred) and neglectful of the need for fundamental change. The German Greens characterise this difference in 'green' views as 'realos' (realists or pragmatists who believe people still want high living standards and that this may be possible) versus 'fundos' (fundamentalists who reject this view — see Papadakis, 1984). 'Reds' criticise all 'greens' for neglecting class and social equity issues (an assertion which is not wholly justified, in my view), for failing to develop realistic alternative institutions and for overlooking political realities. I partly concur with the latter two assertions and suggest below that 'green' and 'red' approaches can be tailored together into a complementary programme.[55]

• 'DEEP GREEN' — ALL CREATURES GREAT AND SMALL

'Deep greens' are at the radical end of the environmentalist spectrum and, though diverse in their perspectives as is the wont of idealists, they generally regard 'light greens' as unadventurous reformers of a bad system, much as revolutionary socialists regard social democratic reformists. Though they may accept a few tenets of the 'externalities', 'commons', 'power' and 'ethical' approaches to environmental analysis, they prefer what I will designate an 'ecological consciousness' approach, a term which appears frequently in the 'deep green' literature. This means that 'deep greens' trace environmental problems to humans' lack of basic ecological consciousness and to their predilection for dominating other species and exploiting natural resources. As a solution 'deep greens' want a reversal of this. They are often dismissed by detractors as extremist, uncompromising, 'fundo' (fundamentalists), romantic, mystical, unrealistic and so forth, but I argue that their message and philosophical orientation must be taken seriously.

The 'deep green' movement par excellence is Deep Ecology which was founded by Norwegian philosopher Arne Naess, developed extensively by US conservationist Bill Devall, and is now active in Europe, North America and Australia. Naess uses the word 'deep' to tactfully distinguish his line from the 'shallower' or 'light green' view, which focuses on surface problems for human benefit rather than on underlying causes. He sometimes speaks of his activities as 'the deep, long-range ecology movement'. Devall calls Deep Ecology a resistance movement against human domination over Nature. Naess regards the two fundamental pillars of Deep Ecology as — a. biocentrism (others call it ecocentrism), or the moral equivalence of all species, plant and animal, as opposed to anthro-pocentrism (priority to human interests); b. Self-realistion, or the holistic consciousness of an expanded Self in relation to the whole of existence, the virtue of which is to render people non-materialistic and minimally demanding of the environment.

Naess and George Sessions have devised a 'platform' of eight basic Deep Ecology principles including, in brief, the following: — all life-forms have intrinsic value; non-human life-forms have value independently of their utility for humans; humans have no right to reduce the richness and diversity of life-forms; current human activity is adversely affecting other life-forms; human societies should pursue quality rather than quantity and the long-term reduction of human populations (for a full list — Naess, 1989:29; Milbrath, 1989:61). Naess advocates that people should formulate a personal 'ecosophy' (ecological philosophy) and set their own values within the Deep Ecology framework. His 'ecosophy' emphasises the unity of life within diversity of forms and the need for a lifestyle compatible with this, including: — anti-consumerism; use of simple systems; preference for intrinsic values; rejection of the luxurious and the unnecessarily novel; preservation of ethnic and culturval diversity; the seeking of work which is meaningful and gentle on Nature; satisfaction of basic needs rather than desires; cultivation of community and non-violent resolution of conflicts. Naess often concludes this sort of listing with the invocation to 'tread lightly on the Earth'.

Most 'deep greens' reject dualism (mind-body separation), which they see as being entrenched in the West by empirical science, in favour of mind-body holism or other spiritual concepts of the East and of various traditional peoples (eg. see Suzuki, 1990a). The outcome is a reversal of the standard Western ordering which holds that action leads to consciousness, towards the view that right consciousness leads to right actions. This does not make 'deep greens' apolitical *per se*, for many are active protesters and a few engage in 'ecotage' (sabotage of ecologically damaging industries), notably the controversial Earth First group in the US. But they largely eschew conventional politics, preferring direct and demonstrative action to raise people's ecological consciousness, thus endeavouring to shift consumer demand away from excessive exploitation of Nature. At present 'deep green' action consists mainly of philosophical argumentation, publication and 'grass roots' organisation. 'Deep green' perspectives are more spiritual than those of other 'greens', though not usually in a conventional sense, and some have even developed new Nature-centred rituals. Some 'deep greens' see themselves as part of an ancient but universal spiritual tradition which has largely been lost by the West in its rush for material affluence, a factor they see as perhaps the main cause of today's environmental crisis.[56]

By and large 'deep green' movements have avoided developing detailed economic programmes, although they are critical of 'blue' and 'light green' policies for the valuation of natural assets, which they see as 'paradoxical' and conducive to anthropocentric instrumentalism. For 'deep greens' true ecological consciousness would in itself reduce Nature-damaging human actions. Where 'blues', many 'reds' and some 'light greens', would give top priority to reducing the environmental or social costs of economic activity through innovation, taxes or regulation (the 'blue shift' of Arrow 1 — Box 4), 'deep greens' tend towards reducing the total damage by cutting demand or even eliminating entire industries if necessary (the 'green shift' of Arrow 2, Box 4). The basic 'deep green' attitude towards human economic activity is nicely encapsulated by one of its slogans — 'simple in means, rich in ends'. Although few 'deep greens' have analysed growth technically, their proposals would seem to imply its demise in the not-too-distant future. They are much more sceptical about technological solutions to environmental problems than are 'light greens', many of whom see value in certain new technologies, including microelectronics.

In conjunction with people of various other 'green' persuasions, many 'deep greens' are developing stimulating new ideas such as: — formation of co-ops for ecologically sound enterprises; organic and non-packaged food retailing; organic agriculture; 'ethical' investment (investment trusts which support only ecologically and ethically sound activities); 'local employment and trade systems' (LETS — an informal trading scheme based on barter or even an unofficial local currency); community energy re-development programmes; urban gardens; recycling promotion schemes; sustainable rural re-development schemes; and 'bioregionalism' (the notion of community and local administration centring in regions of floral, faunal and cultural commonality). These ideas parallel the Third World 'green villages' model I referred to earlier, many 'deep greens' being admirers of Gandhian or other community-based models. Many 'deep greens' see the emergence of the 'hidden' or 'underground' economy in Western countries as an incipient repudiation of economic centralism or 'giantism', and hope to tap these forces into a more de-centralised society (Papadakis, 1984:114ff).

Few 'deep greens' have formulated systematic utopian visions, although some have made utopia-like proposals akin to those of early anarchists such as Kropotkin. Most notable is the work of Edward Goldsmith and the *Ecologist* group, who want almost total de-industrialisation of society by: — inversion of the individualistic values of the industrial revolution; the creation of more appropriate labour-intensive technologies; the decentralisation of social structures back to families and communities; the de-accumulation of capital; a reduced scale of production; the restructuring of production so as to eliminate ecologically damaging activities. This would be implemented by government departments via taxes on raw materials, short-life products or inappropriate technologies and by forcing excessive consumer products off the market. In time, reliance on public welfare and state power would decline, so governance would shrink to a Gandhian system of loosely federated village republics. Claims that this model may revive sexism, generate 'eco-fascism' or exacerbate class differences have, in my opinion, little basis, although some of the Eastern spiritual traditions which some 'deep greens' admire have hierarchical structures. 'Deep greens' believe that such a model would provide equal opportunities for all and minimise class by creating shared communal assets, a claim which I believe to be valid.[57]

As is often the case with idealistic movements which give first priority to consciousness-raising, the immediate group objectives of 'deep greens' are fuzzy and they have poorly developed positions on day-to-day political, social and welfare issues, though this need not be true of individuals. As the 'deep green' movements are not political parties this may not be a handicap at present, but, like the radical Left today, they risk political isolation if the hoped-for revolution in consciousness fails to materialise in the time anticipated. However, 'deep greens' are socially active, they arguably are influencing policies on a number of environmental issues, they may have been partly instrumental in 'blue' economists accepting the notions of 'existence' and 'bequest' value (even though 'deep greens' themselves reject the monetisation of these) and generally they have probably deepened the environmental debate. Feminists and other such groups which advocate fundamental attitudinal change have had a good deal of success during the past two decades in raising consciousness of critical social issues, and 'deep greens' could do likewise.

• HOW GREEN IS YOUR RED?

Various combinations of the above colours are possible and today most political activists would accept some pollution taxes, some planning, some environmental protection and some green consciousness-raising without any qualms. Parties of the moderate Left easily embrace elements of 'light blue', 'light red' and 'light green', although at present there is a convergence on 'light-to-medium blue'. Environmental movements and Green parties now have progressive planks on social welfare, income redistribution, democratisation and public enterprise, ironically, just as many middle-of-the-road Labour and Social Democratic parties are abandoning theirs. Socialist groups now have obligatory green planks.

In my view, however, such vague eclecticism will not be adequate for dealing with deteriorating social and environmental situations in the long-term. Instead I advocate two propositions: — first, rejection of the main elements of capitalist machine-chemical models and 'blue' solutions to environmental problems (with the exceptions noted later); second, adoption of a clearly-defined sustainability concept based on a combination of 'green' and 'red' approaches. I propose this combination because in my view the 'power' approach is the most valid for explaining and solving economic and social problems, while the 'ethical' and particularly the 'ecological consciousness' approaches are the most valid for environmental solutions. I place 'green' foremost because ecological sustainability must become the core value of all socio-economic systems. This combination would require some reconciliation between 'red' and 'green' positions.

At present the chief differences between 'red' and 'green' regarding general environmental and social issues are that, relative to 'green', 'reds': — tend to see environmental problems as serious rather than urgent; are more likely to hold that human activity inevitably modifies ecosystems; are more inclined to accept growth and ecologically dubious industries if these present job opportunities; are more favourable to centralised systems; are more wedded to working class and trade union traditions; are more intent on seeking class-based agents for social change; are less concerned about population pressure; are more inclined to accept industrialism and to hold that industrial development is a prerequisite for socialism; are more prone to anthropocentrism and are less convinced of the need for ecological consciousness or spiritual renewal, many 'reds' being philosophical materialists.

On the other hand, the 'red' and 'green' literature seems to agree on the following: — the need for extensive public intervention in the economy; the desirability of alternative property forms such as co-ops and at least some public enterprise; the need for social equity and limitation of income differentials; concerns about the dangers of some technologies; the virtues of energy conservation; scepticism about the supposed virtues of free trade and the emerging global division of labour; top priority to meeting basic needs and avoidance of excessive luxury; extension of democracy and participatory systems; concern about social alienation and cultural decline; anti-militarism and the need for some international co-operation. Most of the 'green' experimental concepts mentioned earlier are compatible with socialist principles broadly interpreted. Reconciliation would require 'reds' to acknowledge the various limits to growth and the urgency of the environmental crisis, to be less enamoured of industrialism or materialism and to accept that environmental problems will have to be solved long before capitalism spontaneously collapses, if it ever does. 'Greens' would have to seek the ultimate abandonment of capitalism as we currently know it and to adopt more coherent policies on economic, social, welfare and industrial relations issues. Both would have to accept pluralism of religious and philosophical perspectives. Not all 'reds' and 'greens' would accept such a reconciliation, but I believe that many could.

The question still remains of how 'green' should 'red' become — greenish tinges or 'deep green'? My view is that it should be reasonably 'deep green' and that this is commensurate with elements of the conservator 'red' tendency. There have been 'deep green-reds' in the past. One example is the late E. F. Schumacher, who wanted less emphasis on private enterprise and new forms of social ownership, along with profound spiritual renewal, although he once quipped that 'socialism is of interest solely for its non-economic values and the possibility it creates for the overcoming of the religion of economics' (Schumacher, 1973:237). Arguably another 'deep green-red' is former East German Marxist Rudolf Bahro who, if less spiritual than many 'deep greens', wants the wholesale de-industrialisation of Western economies in order to prevent further environmental decay, and he is actively promoting new forms of communal living.

More speculatively, I suggest that if Tawney were still with us he too would be a 'deep green-red'. Not only did he condemn capitalist inequality, functionless private property, urban despoilation and worker alienation, but he was also concerned about the growing social dismissal of religion and about an economy which panders primarily to 'temporary appetites'. He suggested that 'industry itself has come to hold a position of exclusive predominance among human interests, which no single interest, and least of all the provision of the material means of existence, is fit to occupy' (Tawney, 1921:190).

Both 'deep reds' and 'deep greens' seek fundamental changes in human consciousness, though in very different spheres. Both have tended to believe that enlightenment in their respective spheres of concern would automatically bestow sensibility in all other spheres, perhaps an unwise presumption on both sides. The experience of recent decades has been a sobering one for those 'deeper reds' who seek radical social transformation, as the workers have failed to become 'grave diggers' for capitalism and some socialists even fear a dissolution of the working class. I suspect that some class-based dissidence will continue, but that a revival of revolutionary solidarity is unlikely, due to the dispersed nature of dissident forces today. The CPS model appears to be non-viable and is on the verge of collapse. Global depression, the demise of capitalism and nuclear holocaust remain possible but increasingly improbable, while environmental crises are already occurring. In the near future the environmental crisis will be the central issue of world-wide concern though not, of course, the only one. The new consciousness to which socialists have always looked as a force for change must in large measure be shaped by the need to seek solutions to this environmental crisis, and I argue that a mix of 'green–red' concepts provide the best basis for such solutions.

6 ECSSOS AND THE 'GREEN–RED' MODEL

IN Chapter 4 I suggested that the current debate about SD has been unhelpful and that the best-known proposal for SD, which I call the Pearce-WCED model, is inadequate, in spite of its acceptance by some 'greens' (eg. Hare et al, 1990). At the urging of the environmental movement the term 'ecologically sustainable development' (ESD) is now being commonly used in Australia. Whilst this term has its educational merits at present, I suggest, for two reasons touched upon in Chapter 4, that it is not the ideal concept: — first, the word 'development' may be misused and should be avoided; second, the qualification of 'ecological' may be unnecessarily limiting because some environmental problems are now so serious that the machine-chemical economy may not be sustainable in any important respect — whether ecologically, economically or socially. Some studies have proposed a wider and more sophisticated approach, one colourfully advocating a *menage à trois* beween ecological, economic and social dimensions (Crawford et al, 1991).

In the spirit of the last-mentioned approach I propose that all societies should seek 'ecologically and socially sustainable organisations of systems' (ECSSOS), rather than development and growth *per se*. This means that all sub-systems of a society must be organised for sustainability in all respects, but with priority to the ecological and social dimensions. I will refer to this concept specifically as ECSSOS and more generally as 'sustainability'. For brevity I will usually refer to this as the 'substainably organised systems' (SOS) approach. SOS would provide a sustainability framework without being prescriptive of all institutions and policies, so that there would be room for individual variation among societies and ideologies. The 'green-red' model I will sketch should help construct the SOS framework and then provide a basis for some of its more detailed structures. The rest of this chapter outlines the four proposed components or tiers of SOS and a 'green–red' model based thereon. The four components are: — sustainability principles; ecological rules; systemic goals; instruments and institutions.

• SUSTAINABILITY PRINCIPLES

Most of these principles are based on issues discussed earlier and my proposal is that all decision-making in all societies at all times must be centrally guided by them.

i.   Preservation of ecosystems — the central principle of all societies should be the preservation of ecosystems in a state which ensures the integrity of the biosphere.

ii.   Maximum quality and diversity — the number and diversity of species should be maintained at the maximum possible.

iii. Long-term perspectives — all time-span assumptions should be posited on the basis of as long-term a perspective as is required to fulfil the first two principles and to maximise inter-generational equity.

iv.   Risk averseness — where there is ecological uncertainty decision-making should err on the side of environmental caution, particularly where the decisions might be irreversible.

v.   Growth as residual — rates of growth of physical inputs or outputs should not be a goal *per se* but should be a residual outcome only after all other sustainability principles have been taken into consideration.

vi.   Global unity in diversity — decisions should be made in a global context where necessary while maintaining maximum possible local, regional, ethnic and cultural autonomy and diversity, including the preservation of cultural and spiritual traditions.

vii. Optimum population and consumption — population and per capita consumption should be set at levels which are compatible with all other sustainability principles, even if this entails reduction of the present levels in the long-term.

viii. Ecocentrism — all cultural values should begin with respect for all other species and for the integrity of the biosphere; despite our special abilities, humans should be seen as subject to ecological laws, not as an exempt species with priority over other species; the beauty, complexity and diversity of Nature should be retained in its own right, not just for human use.

ix. Democratic control — all decision-making regarding resource usage and technological change should involve, and consider the opinions of, as many people as possible.

x. Social Justice — within the context of all other sustainability principles, policy-making should aim for the maximum possible human rights and social justice in all respects for all people, while adequately meeting basic human needs.

The key implication of these principles is that maintenance of ecosystems, or the 'biocommunity' as some call it (see Milbrath, 1989:Ch.4), should be the core value of all systems. Social equity and social justice should also be included, both in principle and because breaches thereof can force people into behaviour which is damaging to the environment. Cultural and spiritual aspects must be included because these underlie all other dimensions. Where there are environmental constraints on the expansion of human activity it is the growth of population and per capita consumption which should be curtailed, not social justice, income equality or inter-generational equity. These principles should, in time, be written into the constitutions, laws and policy-making procedures of all societies.

• ECOLOGICAL RULES

If ecosystem maintenance is to be the core value of all systems and of human activity as a whole, there will need to be some technical rules of conduct based on current scientific knowledge.

From the large corpus of ecological information available at present the following generalisations can be made, and appropriate rules should be based thereon:

i.   Everything is connected to everything else — ecosystems are so inter-linked that some pollutants are now found in all parts of the Earth and all humans have DDT in their bodies. Our production and disposal policies must be constrained by this.

ii.   Nature works largely through closed-loop cycles, whereas almost all human systems have unclosed linear systems which dump all manner of wastes into otherwise balanced ecosystems. Thus, all human systems must be progressively converted to a closed-cycle basis.

iii.   All energy and matter are entropic so that even recycling is limited. Conservation must, therefore, be the basis of all resource usage, and energy efficiency should be a major economic criterion.

iv.   All ecosystems, including the Earth itself, have maximum carrying capacities, so that populations and other impositions must work within these.

v.   All food chains are subject to 'biomagnification', or increasing concentrations towards the top of the chain, and humans are at the top of most such chains on which they rely. Hence, pollution at the lower levels must be kept to an absolute minimum.

vi.   Changes in ecosystems are complex and can be slow moving, so that solutions may have extremely long lead-times. All policy-making must take this into account.

vii.   By and large ecosystems require diversity, and humans likewise may need ecological diversity for their quality of life and for the survival of both themselves and the biosphere.

viii. There are limits to the ability of ecosystems to absorb intrusions, including human-made pollutants and wastes. This absorbtive capacity may be next-to-nil in the case of some toxic synthetics or genetically engineered organisms which have never before existed. We should therefore take extreme precautions with such substances and preferably avoid their creation altogether.

ix.   There are no synthetic substitutes for some natural products and so the risk of total depletion should be avoided and the concept of extensive 'capital compensation' is not valid.

Many other such generalisations, and rules deducible therefrom, are possible and should periodically be formulated. Extensive scientific research must be devoted to identifying these various rules and monitoring their implementation. All economic planning and regulation of economic activities must take these rules, along with the sustainability principles, as a starting point.

• SYSTEMIC GOALS

These principles and rules must be taken as a basis for formulating the goals of all systems and sub-systems — i.e. all industries, products, resource extraction, energy sources, agriculture, technologies, population policy, cultural values and social policy, as well as for the economy as a whole. A variety of goals are possible and there is room for choice. Some of the goals proposed in the sustainability literature include — appropriateness, flexibility, safety, dependability, resilience, smallness, decentralised structures, efficiency, security, knowledge-enhancement, 'human scale', local control, self-reliance (both individually and nationally), participation, freedom-enhancement, egalitarianism, cultural integrity, social usefulness, non-violence, peace-inducement and many more. Individual or collective ideas and ideologies may guide goal-selection, so long as they are consistent with the sustainability principles and ecological rules.

In the case of agriculture, for instance, Conway has suggested four systemic goals — productivity, stability, sustainability and equitability — while Holling has proposed three similar goals for all natural systems (Barbier, 1989:47ff). For the macro-economy, conventional textbook goals are internal balance (minimum inflation and unemployment) and external equilibrium (minimum overseas debt and trade imbalances). Eventually, however, goal-setting will have to be even more comprehensive than this, with most industries being required to consider the main ecological, social and cultural impacts of both inputs used and outputs made. Enforcing such goals will require the development of sophisticated new systems for public planning, monitoring, impact analysis and what some call 'social auditing'. These may sound intrusive, and business interests are likely to baulk at them initially, but in principle they only involve an extension of processes such as financial auditing and environmental impact analysis which are now accepted. In Australia, business itself is seeking formal protection in the guise of 'resource security' legislation, a device which may prove environmentally damaging and socially divisive through the locking-in of legally sanctioned practices which are ecologically unsound and unpopular. More generally, I am proposing that systemic goal-setting should be driven less by economics or technology and more by ecology, culture and equity considerations.

• INSTRUMENTS AND INSTITUTIONS

As with goal-setting, there must be room in the selection of instruments and institutions for choice and variation based on factors such as cultural preferences, ideologies or social traditions. The prime SOS requirement is that all instruments and institutions be directed towards systemic goals, which in turn are shaped by sustainability principles and ecological rules. Possible instruments and institutions are many, including: — a range of traditional and new economic policies, taxes, regulations, laws, prohibition of certain activities and products, management systems, planning processes, markets, property rights and property-holding systems, social contract systems, alternative technologies, policy integration systems, research, modelling and a full array of socio-cultural policies. The following is a brief survey of some major instruments and institutions required and their Australian implications.

☐ INTEGRATED ENVIRONMENTAL POLICY-MAKING
This is likely to require a mix of regulations and the various categories of market-based instruments discussed in Chapter 5. It will also require new policy-formulation and monitoring systems so that all major government and private sector decisions are based on appropriate systemic goals, preferably integrated nationally through systems of 'green planning' (see below). The key institution for integration would be a national EPA

responsible for pollution control, impact assessment, advice on pollution taxes and levels, ecological reconstruction, general environmental advice and international environmental liaison. In Australia such a body (currently proposed for the Commonwealth level but not yet established) would also liaise with State EPAs, the RAC, all conservation and environment related ministries and any further planning bodies established in due course. All such bodies must be furnished with more resources than they have at present, and the Commonwealth must retain all requisite environmental powers. The many possible instruments include the following:

- An integrated Commonwealth environment and conservation act, enforced by a national EPA and covering the sorts of issues to be outlined below.

- A comprehensive set of 'environmental taxes' on pollution, excessive resource usage and other social costs. Examples might include — taxes or charges on all major pollutants; taxes on all non-renewable resources and energy (Daly suggests it be at a rate which makes renewable alternatives competitive); a 'carbon tax' on fossil fuels (and perhaps on other GHGs); taxes or other penalties on land clearance; higher charges for use of land, water and forests to accurately reflect all environmental costs.

- A set of regulations closely linked to the above-mentioned environmental tax system for use where taxes prove ineffective, including the outlawing or restricting of ecologically undesirable substances or practices.

- A variety of facilitatory instruments (my term) aimed at particular goals, including green procurement policies by governments; measures which promote local and export markets for recycled materials; removal of tax anomalies which are unfriendly to the environment; tax concessions or other subsidies to encourage home insulation or other passive solar building designs; subsidies for energy-saving or environment-improving innovations which are not currently price competitive (eg. cars, refrigerators or light globes); charges on plastic bags to encourage BYO shopping containers; penalties on low durability products.

- A range of adaptive planning instruments (my term) such as seed-funding of local and regional environment programmes (as with the current Landcare projects); infrastructure provision (waste exchanges, recycling centres, reverse vending machines, etc.); standard-setting for building design; community mobilisation for re-vegetation campaigns; promotion of public transport; urban re-design for energy reduction; a national energy labelling system; green consumer advisory services (many green products are fakes or exaggerated at present); seed-funding for local non-packaged food co-ops in place of supermarkets; assistance for new organic farming systems and organic food marketing.
- A 'tin tax' (my flippant term) linked to deposit systems so as to encourage the return of any recyclable items (tins, bottles and other containers, tyres, waste oil, batteries, car bodies and so on).
- A streamlined system for environmental impact assessment so as to minimise delays, uncertainties and costs and to make environmental policies reasonably 'transparent' (see IC, 1990: Appendix 3) whilst still providing adequate protection for the environment.
- Legislated flora and fauna guarantees should have priority over 'resource security' assurance for industry, and a body should be formed to find alternative employment where a development project is over-ruled on environmental grounds.
- The development and use of broad, comprehensive cost-benefit analysis systems for purposes of better environmental impact assessment and environmental planning, with ecological, social and cultural factors being accorded much more weighting than they have received in the past.
- Government-sponsored ethical investment funds for people who want their savings to go into environmentally constructive activities.

Such measures would have to be thoroughly analysed and discussed before being introduced. Major urgent projects to which they might be directed in Australia could include — GHG reduction, energy conservation, reaforestation, reversal of land degradation, waste minimisation and general pollution reduction.

These instruments should be integrated into a long-term 'green plan', which would include new valuation and auditing systems, new national accounts and aggregate modelling systems.

□ PLANNING AND MARKETS

Although I have shed doubt on the efficacy of markets in relation to environmental problems, I am not advocating they be abandoned, and indeed many of the above-mentioned instruments require markets to some extent. On the other hand, however, I argue that much regulation and many new forms of planning will be required. Although planning is currently unfashionable amongst New Right-dominated governments, bureaucracies and advisers and is more difficult than in the past because of economic globalisation, it still has demonstrable validity. Even neo-classical Nobel Laureate Robert Solow has advocated a degree or 'organised indicate planning' for general resource allocation.[58] With Soviet centralised planning fading into history, most countries will henceforth drift towards market-based systems with a variety of public intervention mechanisms, ranging from Scandinavian-style market planning to a new concept of 'market socialism'.

The possible shape of a planning system for Australia is too complex to discuss here, although I have proposed a model elsewhere.[59] A planning system should include both 'top down' structures (for target-setting, implementing, monitoring, etc.) and 'bottom up' structures (for broadly-based participation and advice). Such systems are still used by a number of countries, notably The Netherlands, Norway, Sweden and Japan, who are now re-shaping their planning processes towards environmental ends. A series of 'ecologically sustainable development' working groups are currently devising environmentally-sound economic policies for Australia but these will rely on government discretion for their implementation. Planning documents would normally present guidelines rather than rigid targets, but these can be detailed for the public sector, and government assistance to the private sector can be made conditional upon reasonable compliance.

Planning systems take time and political will to establish, but once formed can be enduring and effective. Many environmental issues are non-monetary, non-valued factors, so a greening economy will need more discretionary planning and less latitude for markets than in the past. This type of planning would be compatible with geographical centralisation of communities and infrastructure which many 'deep greens' and others advocate. If in the very long-run decentralisation of authority were also desired, then this would be possible once SOS values were well established, though some wider economic, environmental and social administration would probably still be required. The planning systems proposed here should be regarded as transitional and their desirability should be regularly reviewed. Some degree of governmental authority is likely to be required for the foreseeable future, in spite of certain interesting libertarian proposals by the anarchist movement, for many purposes including environmental regulation. The nation state is likely to remain the prime unit of administration, also for the foreseeable future, although certain larger, heterogeneous nations may break up, as predicted and advocated by maverick economist Leopold Kohr and as is currently happening with the former federations of the Soviet Union and Yugoslavia.

☐ GREEN RESTRUCTURING AND EMPLOYMENT

At present Australia is developing an industry restructuring programme based on the integration of our economy into the global capitalist machine-chemical economy through a so-called 'level playing field' strategy — i.e. minimisation of tariff and regulatory barriers to trade. Protagonists claim that this will elicit new, globally competitive export-oriented local industries, while detractors fear that it will destroy our existing industrial base without creating a substantial new one. I suspect that the ultimate result will be between the extremities of these prognoses, but well short of the expectations of the free marketeers who champion this programme (see next sub-section), and I believe that many of the potential costs have been ignored.

Instead I advocate a radically different form of industry restructuring based on domestically-focussed 'sustainable' industries, which would be organised consistently with the 'green plan' proposed above. This would differ from the current programme in many respects, but primarily in being centred on SOS requirements and in adjusting demand to these requirements rather than allowing all demands to have their head, as the fashionable market-based ideology of most Western countries prescribes. This approach would, in time, result in what has been called a new economic 'metabolism' (Ayers and Kneese, 1989:107), which would differ dramatically from today's unsustainable machine-chemical economy.

Green restructuring would begin with wide-ranging industry and community consultation, followed by the formulation of a 'green plan' which would set targets such as a sustainable macro output level, sustainable input quantities, ecologically and socially appropriate production techniques and other technologies, a desirable product mix and employment implications. A very basic and experimental version of such a process is currently being undertaken in Australia through a series of so-called Ecologically Sustainable Development (ESD) Working Groups, representing government, business, environmental groups and sundry other interests. These ESD working groups have produced some useful detailed proposals for more environmentally-sound industry development, but they are based on very broad sectors rather than specific industries, they have not elicited a green consensus and they rely heavily on government for implementation of their proposals (see ESD, 1991).

Plans for green restructuring would be implemented with instruments of the sort proposed in the previous two sub-sections, and would include specific goals such as the following: — the cutting of unnecessary production; the elimination of unnecessary or dangerous products; replacement of virgin resources with recycled secondary materials; minimisation of packaging; reduction of transportation; conversion of industry to a basis which can use renewable energy sources; deployment of non-polluting vehicles; replacement of private with public transport; development of 'sustainable life cycle' manufacturing — i.e. all phases based on sustainability principles (see ESD, 1991:88); conversion of agriculture to a predominantly organic basis and all renewable sectors to a sustained yield basis (see ESD, 1991:1-42); refurbishment of Australia's decaying public infrastructure, but with consideration being given to smaller, more ecological alternatives and to whether we need as much infrastructure as in the past (see Dunkley, 1989).

One pioneering case study of a sustainable industry policy — for the Australian pulp and paper sector (Crawford, 1991) — found that a combination of demand reduction policies, varied feedstocks and new 'cleaner' production technologies could render the industry self-reliant (currently we import extensively) and sustainable, with far fewer pulp mills than are being proposed at the moment. This would, however, require public intervention, planning and the cultivation of much more economical paper-use habits. Another example might be the motor vehicle industry, which should be reduced to one publicly-owned firm and restructured so as to produce a limited range of environmentally-sound, highly fuel-efficient local vehicles to replace imports (currently about ten per cent of our total import bill). This should be done in conjunction with a demand management programme aimed at improving public transport and reducing the need for cars, thereby helping to staunch the explosion of 'motorisation' which is occurring world-wide (Pappas, 1990:194).

Another key candidate for green restructuring would be agriculture as it becomes increasingly clear that machine-chemical farming is unsustainable. Restructuring would involve a shift both to more environmentally sound techniques and to products which are amenable to their use. Techniques of 'whole farm planning' and organic agriculture are well established and are gradually spreading world-wide. Organic methods employ new versions of traditional practices such as inter-cropping, crop rotation, companion planting, use of natural manures, non-tillage and multi-species systems, thereby largely eschewing chemicals or biotechnology, minimising habitat disturbance and preserving soil quality. Such methods can be used for self-reliance, for commercial production and in conjunction with wider energy-efficient community systems, as with the concept of 'permaculture' which was devised in Australia by Bill Mollison and David Holmgren.

Relative to machine-chemical farming, organic agriculture appears, from currently available evidence, to achieve somewhat lower labour productivity, almost comparable per acre yields and considerably higher productivity per unit of energy used. The Japanese 'natural farming' guru, Masanobu Fukuoka, claims that the entire population of Japan could survive well on small farms and in largely self-reliant communities using his methods. Organic agriculture movements in the UK are advocating that some twenty per cent of British farm land be worked organically by the year 2000 and that government seek such a target. A US study, using tentative data, has found that if all US agriculture were converted to pre-Second World War organic standards production would decline slightly, prices would rise and exports would fall to meet domestic requirements, but that production costs would be lower and farm incomes higher except in some less fertile regions. This and other evidence suggests that an organic alternative is quite feasible but would entail substantial restructuring and new lifestyles.[60] The world now spends some US$300 billion per annum on subsidies to machine-chemical agriculture, an industry which is heavily polluting and arguably unsustainable. This level of expenditure should be reduced and much of it re-directed to assist with conversions to organic agriculture.

Green restructuring would occur at both the micro level, as with the examples outlined in the previous paragraphs, and at the macro level as new sustainable industries are sought and all industries are locked into ECSSOS-based planning. This may involve some attempt by governments or other authorities at 'picking winners' among alternative industries, a concept which is anathema to the New Right and other free marketeers. By and large, however, most green restructuring would entail the more modest and feasible aims of meeting old demands in new ways, limiting unsustainable demands, changing market conditions (eg. by requiring organic standards for food production) and creating new markets (eg. by compelling use of recycled materials). The final result would be a dramatically different type of economy as new demands emerged and multiplier effects radically changed direction. A shift to organic agriculture, for instance, would virtually eliminate a range of highly damaging capital-, energy- and chemical-intensive, import-oriented industries in favour of many new, locally-based, skilled labour-intensive industries and services. As Marx long ago realised, the technologies and modes of production chosen can greatly affect all associated socio-economic systems. This form of agriculture could be adopted by a range of enterprise types ranging from family farms (as is happening in the USA already) to various new farms of co-operative, using a variety of organic practices. Being a new 'mode of production' organic agriculture should be promoted coterminously with any such new property-holding forms, rather than waiting for the latter to emerge as many 'reds' advocate.

Many workers, unionists and 'red' intellectuals are understandably concerned that 'green' policies may destroy jobs, but planned restructuring could ensure that new jobs were regularly created. In fact most research (see Note 62) suggests that environmentally-sound activities can provide a substantial nett increase in employment. The result could be growthless jobs rather than the 'jobless growth' which now often characterises high tech machine-chemical economies.

Green jobs would come from at least three major sources: — first, job shifts (eg. from forestry to recycling and re-use) which may involve nett employment increases where new services are created; second, new environmental industries and services such as manufacturing and installing pollution control equipment (an activity which is now worth US$30 billion per annum in Europe and employs over a million people[61]), planning, system design, modelling, recycling management, materials collection, energy auditing, forestry, biological and ecological research, energy conservation programming, land restoration and many more; third, green employment would normally be much more labour intensive than equivalent current activities, either because services are involved or because of the techniques used. Organic agriculture, for instance, is thought likely to employ more people for about the same output, yield (land productivity) and nett production cost than machine-chemical farming. Thus, if all Australian agriculture went organic, which I believe it eventually should, it could greatly increase agricultural employment, revive country districts and reverse the current rural de-population.[62]

Some greens favour the encouragement of labour intensity through the taxing of capital, resource and energy inputs, and by the redistribution of the revenue as labour subsidies (Daly) or as guaranteed minimum income payments (Gorz and others). I believe that this form of large-scale redistribution on a permanent basis would be impractical and unnecessarily interventionist, and it would rely on revenue sources which most greens want reduced. However, some increased labour intensity and employment potential could be encouraged through selective capital taxes, removal of payroll taxes, promotion of handicraft or other self-reliant employment and requisite regulations (such as requiring agriculture to be organic). All corporate subsidies should be on the basis of jobs created, not capital employed. Of course, 'blues' worry that this would cut productivity, thus reducing living standards, growth potential and international competitiveness. In fact, productivity may not be reduced in all cases and, as noted in Chapter 4, it is already declining in some sectors due to environmental damage, so that green policies might actually raise productivity levels and growth rates. Where productivity is reduced, this will often be the result of ecologically conscious consumers freely choosing lifestyles involving labour-intensive goods and services, most of which are likely to be non-tradeable and would not affect external competitiveness. Moreover, current evidence suggests that competitiveness now derives much less from unit labour costs than in the past (see below), so slightly lowered productivity levels might not significantly affect our trade prospects.

In any case perhaps, as Tawney suggested long ago (Quotation 4, Box 1), we are unduly obsessed with productivity, which after all is just GDP measured against inputs. Productivity-enchancing technological change is the main dynamo of the machine-chemical growth treadmill, not capital accumulation as many Marxists seem to think. In sum, there is every reason to believe that green employment would be more plentiful, healthy, flexible and interesting than that of today's machine-chemical economies. Accompanied by appropriate 'soft' technologies, labour-intensive green employment need not be back-breaking or arduous.

□ THE GREENING OF TRADE

Trade is often called the 'engine of growth' because much, but not all, evidence suggests that strong export expansion boosts economic growth, although environmental, social and cultural costs are never included in this equation. Many expansionist economists are now even claiming that export-led industrialisation will help the environment by taking pressure off resources (such as forests) and by depositing people safely in cities. A number of countries, including Australia and many developing countries, are therefore now seeking new export-led growth through freer trade and 'clever' technology-based internationally competitive products. An influential exponent of this view is the US competitiveness theorist, M. E. Porter (1990), who claims that it is more competitive and profitable to shift from 'resource-driven' sectors to 'investment-driven' and 'innovation-driven' activities through knowledge-based goods and services. His suggestion that strong environmental policies can increase competitiveness because importers are now greenishly discerning (Porter, 1990:648) has inspired some Australian 'light greens', who also suggest that environmental services might become a 'cutting edge' sector for export growth.

I have grave reservations about this rosy picture. As regards developing countries, it over-estimates low income as a cause of environmental problems, irresponsible industrial development being a more important cause, and it also over-estimates the benefits of both exports and growth. The much-admired models of Taiwan and South Korea contain the appalling flaw that they have required a massive boost to agricultural productivity via huge energy and chemical inputs, thus leaving an horrendous legacy of pollution, community breakdown and cultural decay. Yet these countries are now being thwarted in their attempts to introduce more sophisticated industries by their reliance on TNCs whose preferred export centres are elsewhere. In Ireland a similar model based on TNC chemical industries has gained few jobs, has damaged local industries such as fishing, has created a serious pollution problem and has provoked strong community resistance.[63]

Many newly industrialising countries are creating cheap labour havens and pollution havens in order to attract TNC capital, these including China, the once great idealist. The evidence suggests that this strategy can attract certain industries, but that it is unreliable, creates major social costs and leaves the society dependent on location decisions by TNCs. Some rich countries fear losses of industries to pollution-havens and so advocate 'green tariffs' or less stringent environmental controls. I support 'green tariffs' if necessary, but the evidence suggests that pollution-havens have too little effect on global trade, investment and comparative advantage to warrant diluting high environmental standards, which can in fact bring competitive benefits in an increasingly environment-conscious world (Leonard, 1988; Porter,

1990:648; Economist, 1990:25). A strong case can be made that all countries should pursue modest development based on locally-funded, small, clean industries which benefit citizens and maintain communities.

Some current restructuring proposals in Australia sound ominously like a modified pollution-haven strategy. The Prime Minister (Hawke, 1989) has claimed the right to continue transport growth and other GHG-producing activities in the name of competitiveness, while the Garnaut Report and the BCA (1990:17) have advocated minerals processing and other high pollution industries for which we allegedly have comparative advantage because of our low population density. The government's strategy at present is to generate 'high value added' goods or 'elaborately transformed manufactures' plus some knowledge-intensive goods and services through free trade, 'level playing fields', 'multi-function polises' and other forms of erudition. The aims of this trade restructuring programme are to reduce our heavy dependence on primary exports and their allegedly weakening prices, to develop a more sophisticated export base, to increase the traded share of GDP and to foster what one government adviser, Helen Hughes, has called an 'export culture'. This supposedly requires new technical education and training systems, computer literacy, an outward-looking, competitive mentality and so forth, so that we can soon transform ourselves into a 'clever country'.

Some commentators agree with these objectives but are sceptical about the methods, pointing to current evidence that competitiveness in sophisticated industries derives from factors such as quality, knowledge, skills, networking or complementary 'clusterings' of firms, most of which can be promoted by government through a 'strategic' industry policy. This view is hotly disputed but experience in many European and Asian countries suggests that some industry promotion is possible, although Porter (1990), who is often cited on the matter, actually says that promotion is more successful for 'investment-driven' industries than for 'innovation-driven' sectors. Many unionists support this 'strategic trade promotion' approach because they think it will create sophisticated new sectors of employment and get us away from being a mere 'offshore quarry' for richer industrial countries. Various union leaders and 'red' intellectuals think such a strategy may re-industrialise Australia and revive a flagging manufacturing sector, which they see as essential for constantly growing rich country living standards. Some environmentalists support this strategy because they believe that it will enable us to diversify production and exports away from environmentally damaging resource and agriculture sectors (eg. Hare, 1990).

Other commentators largely approve of the government's restructuring method but foresee a different result. They see merit in reducing protection and improving inefficiencies, but believe that we could not compete in many new sectors of 'elaborately transformed manufactures' or high technology because we lack sophisticated domestic markets or competitive 'world-scale' companies and because these sectors have a very small base. Commentators holding this view therefore believe that Australia must continue to rely on agricultural and resource exports well into the foreseeable future, if not forever.[64] The Industries Commission, the Commonwealth Government's chief advisory body on industry policy, has questioned whether commodity prices are sufficiently unstable as to warrant a panic shift away from primary exports,[65] and for reasons I discussed in Chapter 4, commodity prices may rise in future. Commonwealth Treasurer, John Kerin, has candidly warned that TNCs based in Australia would be unlikely to let us become an export platform (*Age*, 5 January 1991), a remarkable confirmation of what 'red' critics of global dependence have been saying for many years.

By and large, however, there is a mainstream consensus that Australia needs to become more export-oriented by greatly reducing (if not wholly eliminating) protection levels, globalising our economy, abolishing unnecessary regulations, cutting costs through efficiency improvements in sectors such as transport, communications, ports and the labour market and generally becoming a 'clever' country. The broad object of this exercise is to reduce our chronic trade deficit, moderate our massive external debt, increase our national wealth and accelerate the growth of our living standards. There are some marginal dissenters from this consensus, such as those who advocate retention of a modicum of protection and export promotion (eg. Pappas, 1990), or those who, like Professor J. D. Pitchford, think that our external debt is not a problem because it is manageable, is not unprecedented and will eventually be self-reducing.

I take issue with most premises, objectives and methods of this consensus view, although I do not share Pitchford's opinion that debt does not matter. In recent years our nett foreign debt has been around a third of GDP, costing us three per cent of GDP and 20 per cent of export revenue to service. When foreign equity ownership is included, foreign liabilities are almost half our GDP, costing four per cent of GDP and a quarter of export revenue to service. In some years repayment of principal and interest together have cost ten per cent of GDP and an incredible 60 per cent or more of export revenue (Reserve Bank *Bulletin*, December issue annually). Even if this is technically sustainable, it represents a highly undesirable use of our resources and forces us into policy measures and directions of development which may be questionable from environmental, social and cultural points of view.

My disagreement with the consensus view is based on several grounds. First, I dispute the conventional assumption that our external indebtedness is caused primarily by our trade deficit, which in turn is caused by our uncompetitiveness. Although this causal sequence is not untrue it is over-simplified. Other major, and perhaps more important, causes of our debt include: — the explosion of global speculative financial movements; excessive de-regulation; corporate preference for debt; undue reliance on high interest rates for macro policy-making; excessive government borrowing for consumption purposes; tax distortions which favour debt borrowing; official encouragement of entrepreneurial speculation (not long ago just four entrepreneurs were responsible for over ten per cent of our foreign debt — *Age,* 25 October 1989) and various other such structural factors, all of which came to a head in the 1980s.

Second, I dispute the standard attribution of our trade deficit primarily to our alleged uncompetitiveness, although high costs and above-average inflation (until recently) play some role. Equally, if not more, important is the fact that we are heavily dependent on imports for a vast range of goods and services such as: — capital equipment, technology, defence hardware, cultural items (especially US TV programmes), transportation, insurance and so forth. The largest deficit items in our trading account is the 'invisibles' component, which includes debt servicing payments, repatriation of company dividends, freight and insurance. I will refer to this as our 'structural dependence' problem. The result is that, in technical terms, we have a very high 'marginal propensity to import' (i.e. any growth in demand swiftly and substantially boosts imports) and inordinately low 'elasticity of demand' for imports (i.e. price rises do not deter our import demand, so exchange rate changes are not as effective at reducing our trade deficit as the textbooks suggest).

My third disagreement with the consensus view, and with the current restructuring programme, is that trade de-regulation and integration into the world economy may have unanticipated adverse consequences, or may even backfire. There is substantial evidence that a country's export prospects in 'elaborately transformed manufactures' and high technology sectors depend more on research, quality, a domestic base, servicing, networking and so forth, rather than on labour costs or other traditional measures of competitiveness (eg. see Porter, 1990; Pappas, 1990). For Australia this means that it is market development rather than micro-economic reforms which will count and that, whilst we may find a few market niches, the idea of us becoming a major trader in sophisticated manufactures is probably a pipedream. Our current base in these products is too small, we are too inexperienced and we may have missed the boat. I therefore agree with those (Note 64) who hold that we will remain dependent on agricultural and mineral exports for a long time to come. On the other hand, however, the currently required rates of expansion in these areas are certain to have serious environmental impacts and are likely to elicit continuing conflict over resource issues.[66]

My final disagreement with the current consensus view is that the underlying rationale of raising national wealth and living standards is misplaced. For reasons which I touched on earlier and will further amplify below, I argue that conventional measures of wealth and living standards are questionable. In environmental, social and cultural terms our living standards may well be declining, but this will not be helped by a restructuring policy which induces major socio-cultural changes in order to seek a bit more material growth. Our levels of wealth, GDP and national disposable income per capita are still growing steadily, if more slowly than in earlier post-war decades, even though we have slipped relatively to eighteenth in the world.[67] Recent slowdowns in our growth rate have substantially been due to macro contraction by the government in an effort to contain imports. I suggest that we question the virtue of continued material growth in order to struggle a few rungs up the ladder. The frequent assertion that Australia is battling for 'survival' is largely hyperbole and is somewhat misconstrued. Insofar as our survival is threatened it is primarily for ecological, social and cultural reasons.

In short, my main concern is that the purported economic benefits of restructuring, export-orientation and possible higher material living standards have not adequately been set against non-economic costs such as the loss of some national independence, technological or other structural dependency and ecological or socio-cultural impacts of the sort noted in Chapter 4. This question is being widely posed in Europe where the next round of EC integration has been officially estimated as likely to add between 2.5 and 6.5 per cent (some say more) to current total community income, and the most bullish growth estimate suggests an extra one per cent per annum in the long-term. These benefits are likely to be very unequally divided between member countries, and there is a widespread feeling that non-economic costs have not been adequately assessed relative to the, arguably modest, growth benefits. An Australian study found that a halving of world protection would gain Australia and New Zealand US$14 billion together, a few per cent of GDP and much less if spread over many years. Such calculations, which abound at present, are based on highly speculative assumptions.[68]

I do not suggest that there will be no benefits for Australia from low tariffs, global trade stimuli and efficiency-raising exercises in various tardy sectors. What I am questioning is the overall advantage of notions such as global integration, 'export culture' or the 'clever country', whose costs have not been adequately discussed and which have been subject to only cursory public debate. The idea of changing our entire culture in order to balance our trading books would seem to warrant serious questioning. In particular I question the dogmatic adherence to free trade and concomitant de-regulation, as widely advised and apparently now sought by the Hawke Government. Such a doctrine would prevent us from using protection for: — temporary employment purposes, curtailing dumping, excluding environmentally, socially or culturally undesirable products or promoting strategic industries. Dogmatic adherence to a 'level playing field' can result in a situation like that of New Zealand where privatisation, de-regulation and abandonment of protection in the telecommunications sector allowed the new US owners of NZ Telecom to source inputs overseas, thereby devastating the fledgling local telecommunications equipment industry (Davidson, *Age*, 9 March 1991). Prime Minister Bob Hawke claims that the world is de-regulating and that there is pressure on us to follow suit. This is partly true, but some countries have retained appropriate regulations where required, many countries have more hidden forms of protection than we have and exchange rate re-regulation has some support.[69]

I propose that our prime object should be a more ecologically and socially sustainable way of organising trade, and that sustainable trade be an integral part of green restructuring (see above). Rather than an 'export culture' we need an ECSSOS culture, with global trading links only where these are necessary or particularly beneficial. Reduction of a trade deficit can be achieved only through one of three strategies (or a combination thereof) — expansion of existing exports, stimulation of new export items or reduction of imports. So far Australian strategy debates have concentrated solely on the first two options, with imports being treated as a virtual sacred cow, whereas I advocate that much more emphasis be placed on import reduction than has hitherto been contemplated.

If this seems heretical, then it should be remembered that recent government strategy has been to grow more slowly than the rest of the world in order to staunch demand and (indirectly) check imports, a policy which doubtless contributed to the 1990-1 recession and has boosted unemployment. Purists claims that direct restriction of imports is economically inefficient, but many argue that it is more inefficient and inequitable to induce unemployment for the same (indirect) import-reducing purpose. Conservative economists believe that the short-term 'pain' of unemployment is justified by the long-term 'gain' of economic 'shake-out' and post-recession efficiency, but in capitalist business cycles the whole process begins again within a few years. Some Keynesian economists argue that short-term import reduction can be efficient by easing unemployment and demand slumps during a recession, thereby maintaining trade at higher levels than would prevail if a serious depression were allowed to occur.

At present our imports consist roughly of one third consumer goods, one third capital goods and one third other less clear-cut categories. During recent years our current account deficit has been so huge that it would have taken an across-the-board cut in imports of more than one third to rectify it, or the elimination of all imports of vehicles, miscellaneous manufactures, electrical equipment, paper products and sundry other items. Alternatively, cutting all imports of vehicles, petroleum, chemicals and industrial machinery would have largely eliminated the deficit — that is, an instantaneous transformation of the machine-chemical economy.[70] Clearly there is no realistic mix of import reductions which would alone solve our trade deficit problem in the short-term, but in the longer-term import trimming could greatly alleviate the need for environmentally, socially or culturally questionable export expansion. An import reduction strategy would lower our trading ratio and may reduce economic growth or productivity slightly, but the more imports can be reduced the less we need to seek new export ventures or expand resource projects. Mining in environmentally or culturally sensitive areas could thus be avoided and ecologically destructive sectors such as wheat-growing, outback grazing, forest products and farming in over-cultivated or salinated areas could be reduced or eliminated. For social and cultural reasons we should also limit our reliance on tourism, export of education and any goods or services which make us too dependent on imported technologies or expertise.

I propose a ten-point programme for an ecologically and socially sustainable solution to our dual problems of the current account (trade) deficit and external debt, the first three relating to debt-reduction and the rest primarily to trade matters:

i.   Accelerate the retirement of debt whenever possible, and restrict new loan-raisings by public and private sector enterprises. The more rapidly this can be done, the more will debt service payments be cut and the current account deficit trimmed.

ii. Increase the supply of domestic savings through restriction of overseas investment by financial institutions; some directional control over, and strict prudential supervision of, the investments of financial institutions; wider community control over superannuation funds (as in Sweden); savings incentive schemes linked to low cost housing for lower income people (as in Germany and Japan); government-sponsored and supervised ethical investment schemes through which aware people can invest in ecologically and socially sustainable projects; and appropriate tax changes (next point). If such measures were to succeed in substantially raising the national savings ratio, our reliance on overseas sources of debt and equity finance could be greatly reduced, thus enabling us to avoid large debts in future and minimise foreign ownership of our assets. This would alleviate much of present structural dependence problems (see earlier).

iii. Change the tax system so as to avoid tax concessions for corporate debt; income tax on personal savings be graduated so as to exempt lower income people; examine the possibility of taxing expenditure rather than income, a concept which was proposed by a 1978 British Royal Commission (the Meade Report) but never implemented, the purpose being to discourage consumption and foster savings.

iv. Re-regulate the exchange rate so that discretionary depreciation of the currency becomes more practicable than at present. This need not involve firmly fixed rates, which have proved problematic in the past, but may entail 'crawling peg' adjustments or a controlled float with a 'target zone'. This would best be done globally, a notion which is beginning to re-gain favour (see Note 69), but a unilaterally managed rate is possible. A more controlled exchange rate would facilitate more successful depreciation than we can achieve at present for the traditional purpose of encouraging exports, checking imports and stemming our current account deficit. Care must be taken with this measure, however, because at present our demand inelasticity does not favour depreciation, and a lower exchange rate raises the 'passive' component of our external debt. This may be a rather limited instrument for some time to come because of our peculiar structural dependence problem.

v. Adopt a macro-economic policy system which minimises our inflation rate relative to trade rivals while also containing unemployment (see below). If this could be achieved it would render our exports more competitive in the long-run. Many of the current micro-economic and labour market reforms, which are aimed at lower costs, greater efficiency and better competitiveness (see IC, 1990), seem sensible enough and should be persisted with except where labour exploitation, loss of employment security, or other social costs are likely. It remains to be seen whether the world-wide frenzy of de-regulation and privatisation will ultimately bring more efficiency than countervailing inequities and social costs. I remain open-minded but sceptical.

vi. Expand our traditional exports where necessary for current account purposes, but only under strict environmental and heritage guidelines, allowing for reductions where desirable (see above). We should seek to do more processing of our resources in order to retain more 'value added' (and more export revenue) within Australia, but not for the sake of importing other countries' pollution as some actually advocate (see above). A major candidate for value added enhancement should be the wool industry, from which we could readily develop a linked garment industry and an Australian fashion style.

vii. Establish a programme for encouraging new export areas, including, for instance some 'elaborately transformed manufactures'; some high tech products; ecologically and socially sound biotechnologies; wool products; garments; recycled materials and products; environmental and other services; organic agricultural knowledge and products; and 'soft' energy systems. Evidence suggests that new export items should be based on existing or promising domestic industries. These should be fostered through a variety of financial and other incentives, concessional loans, infrastructure assistance, marketing advice and the establishment of networks with complimentary enterprises or products, a concept which has been successful in various parts of the world. Many economists question the efficacy of such measures and free marketeers hotly oppose them, but there is now a good deal of evidence that export success requires a strong domestic base, active marketing, reliable servicing, competitive enterprises, networking with complementary products and possibly some start-up assistance.[71] Certainly there are dangers in such a programme. It may, for instance, disadvantage products which are not assisted, favour politicians' pet projects, foster ecologically or socially unsound activities for the sake of export-generation (as in the case of many newly industrialising countries — see above), or be aimed at bolstering a nationalistic high tech ego. The programme should, therefore, be limited in scope, be associated with low but flexible tariffs, be closely linked with green planning and restructuring and should seek small, specialised niches rather than large-scale glamour industries.

viii. Investigate ways of reducing our 'invisible' (freight, insurance and other services) deficit, perhaps by creating an overseas shipping line, more locally based insurance and other related trading services. However, such developments would have to be carefully costed and could yield benefits only in the longer-term.

ix. Reduce foreign ownership levels through regulation and the promotion of local equity (see ii above), so as to limit dividend repatriation and to prevent the well-known TNC practice of refusing to source exports in peripheral countries like Australia.

x. Conduct an extensive inquiry into the possibilities for import reduction, feasible areas for cut-backs and the methods which might be used. There are three possible forms of import reduction — import substitution (where imports are replaced by equivalent local production); import restriction (where importation is cut off by tariffs or quotas); and import demand management (where demand for certain imports is reduced or eliminated without replacement). All three should be used, but with emphasis on the third, which could be at least partly implemented quite quickly. The main aims of an import reduction programme would be to contract the import side of our current account deficit; to circumvent any propensity towards environmentally and socially unsound exports for the sake of balancing trade; to alleviate our present import dependence in so many sectors; and to lower our currently very high marginal propensity to import (see earlier). The targets, measures and instruments to be used would be as follows:

- temporary across-the-board import duties, but with strict 'sunset' clauses to ensure that the measure is only operated while employment or trade deficit problems persist;

- specific duties targetted at items whose reduction is warranted by SOS principles, such as — luxuries; products which are the result of 'environmental dumping' (my term for items produced at less than full social and environmental cost — eg. rainforest timbers); products derived from the extreme exploitation of labour; products deemed unnecessarily consumerist; and energy imports (currently almost five per cent of our import bill);

- an import substitution programme, in conjunction with green planning and restructuring, aimed at creating or extending local industries or services which could feasibly replace current imports and reduce our high import dependence — eg. certain industrial machinery (currently more than 12 per cent of our import bill), some computers and office equipment (2.5 per cent of our import bill), minimisation of imported television programming and many more;

- a general demand management programme to reduce the demand for imports through conservation, frugality or the development of alternatives: — eg. energy conservation, lower paper-use, alternative technologies, less use of transport, farming methods which cut the use of chemicals (about two per cent of imports) and campaigns to stem addiction to tobacco, coffee and other beverages (about one per cent of imports).

- a variety of programmes to increase savings (see earlier) and reduce consumption, to heighten people's awareness of the need to reduce imports, to ensure that country-of-origin labelling is correct and generally to combat consumerism (see below). Such programmes should encourage Australians to reconsider whether we need so many imports, and should endeavour to combat our structural dependence (see earlier) or our consumerist cultural cringe.

This ten-point programme I have outlined for the reduction of external debt and our current account deficit would need to be closely linked with green planning and restructuring, should be carefully designed and must be closely monitored. It would involve interventionism and a good deal of re-regulation, but it does not imply a simple return to the pre-deregulatory era for it would entail a wide variety of novel objectives and mechanisms. The programme would take some time to establish and certain constituent elements would mainly be applicable only in the long-term, but it is quite practicable and warrants serious consideration.

The main conclusion of this sub-section is that the extreme laissez faire, free market, 'level playing field' approach to trade and industry restructuring, which has gripped our policy-makers today, is dogmatic, is based on an unduly narrow cost-benefit analysis and may have adverse consequences. This approach involves the notion of adjusting policies to a precept (free trade) and allowing economic, social, and cultural consequences to adapt willy nilly. I advocate the reverse sequence that we decide, in the broad, what type of environment, culture, society and economy we want and adapt policies to these ends, but always with thorough cost-benefit analysis. This need not, and should not, mean a return to the old regulatory regime, but a new system based on foresight, a modicum of planning and a wider variety of instruments than hitherto used. This alternative approach should start from SOS precepts, and should include the provision that instruments such as tariffs and other regulations are legitimate but must be limited because of their potential social costs. Protectionist policies of the past have been based on the single-minded, poorly monitored, unplanned and sometimes badly-conceived goal of industrialisation based on the machine-chemical model. My proposed system of green planning and restructuring would be broader and deeper in conception with thorough monitoring. It would mean largely controlling our fate rather than abandoning it to global market forces and TNCs as is our destiny on a 'level playing field'.

☐ A NEW WORLD ORDER FOR WHOM?
Current calls for a 'new world order' based on ever increasing international integration and de-regulation of everything should

be treated with caution. Certainly inter-dependence is substantial and growing, but in a way which requires qualification. A quarter of all world trade is intra-firm (TNCs trading with their own subsidiaries), 60 per cent is intra-industry and three quarters is between the rich OECD countries. This much-vaunted inter-dependence is, therefore, primarily the result of a few 'modern' industries producing goods largely peripheral to basic human needs, plus the energy which powers these industries and the capital which funds them. That is, trade reflects the unsustainable machine-chemical economy. A world of greening economies based on SOS principles, organic agriculture, small sustainable industries, environmental knowledge and social services could, however, greatly reduce dependence on this traded sector.

The new world order currently being proposed by President Bush and other world leaders formally consists of more multilateral co-operation through the UN and freer trade through GATT. However, arguably the more informal agenda is greater economic control by bodies such as the International Monetary Fund (IMF) and the World Bank, particularly over Third World countries, a freer hand for TNCs from rich countries and even more political influence by the US as the Earth's sole super-power. For some years now the Uruguay Round of GATT talks has been negotiating a proposal for more liberalised commodity trade and a largely unpublicised proposal for a General Agreement on Trade in Services (GATS), the latter being aimed at reducing domestic regulations which impede trans-border services. Both proposals contain a complex array of costs and benefits but have been stalled for some time on a range of issues. At the time of writing the GATS proposal, in which Australia has played a leading role, looks like going ahead.

Champions of free trade support both proposals, of course, but critics have expressed a variety of concerns, including the following: Third World development might be impeded (because free trade is thought unfriendly to the less economically developed partners, a view for which there is circumstantial evidence but no firm proof); the position of TNCs may be strengthened; TNC status may be extended to many service enterprises; cultural diversity may be even further eroded; alternative approaches to development may be restricted; no consideration is being given to ecological issues as a factor in trade; import controls for environmental purposes ('green tariffs') may be limited or precluded by new GATT provisions (eg. bans on tropical hardwood imports); de-regulation of agricultural trade may encourage more forest clearance for the US hamburger market; regulatory 'harmonisation' may competitively reduce environmental controls to a global lowest common denominator.

In recent years US-Canadian free trade arrangements have forced the Canadians to adopt the lower US environmental standards and to water down their regulations in various ways. EC free trade arrangements have been used to over-ride Dutch vehicle emission controls and a Danish recycling law. Already GATT rules have been invoked to undermine a Thai government anti-smoking policy and a US ban on tuna imports from Mexico, which was implemented because the Mexican fishing methods were killing dolphins. The latter case appears to have set a precedent which is unfavourable to the use of trade measures for environmental purposes.[72] The current draft of GATS provides for rather loose, flexible arrangements which are sensitive to concerns of Third World countries, allow new domestic regulations, and provide for varying religious or other cultural values. On the other hand, the GATS draft refers to 'a wider process of economic integration among countries', envisages further liberalisation in future and wants eventual extension to all services.[73]

There are obvious benefits from stabilised, less discriminatory services trade but many less obvious dangers, for services such as telecommunications, broadcasting, advertising, education, tourism and so forth (not all of which are covered by the current GATS draft) have far-reaching political, cultural and other social implications. Complete globalisation could well jeopardise cultural diversity, national integrity and the ability of societies to develop radically different social systems, whether for environmental, cultural or even spiritual reasons. Business thinking on such matters is ominous. The *New York Times* has warned that 'the new order eschews loyalty to workers, products ... communities, even the nation', while one US businessman has declared that 'all such allegiances are viewed as expendable under the new rules'.[74] Australia has been a very active animator for a Uruguay Round settlement and for GATS, but there are few indications that the above-mentioned problems have been considered, although Australian negotiators, to their credit, appear to have played a leading role in thwarting US attempts to outlaw local content requirements for television. Problems of the sort mentioned should be given more attention in future.

A number of more ecologically and socially sustainable ways of organising trade arrangements have been proposed (see Ekins, 1986: Ch.14; Robertson, 1989) but these may reduce trade and might well be impossible to implement under a new world order dominated by the USA and rich world TNCs, or with GATT acting as an 'economic policeman'. I suggest that a preferable world order would be a more loosely-knit structure with the following institutions: multilateral collective security through the UN, supplemented by other alliances as desired; an international clearing bank, based on the original Keynes-Schumacher model, in place of the IMF; a world environmental and resources authority to enforce pollution standards, solve ecological problems and manage global common property resources; an international trade organisation to assist with fair inter-country exchange, control TNCs and prevent excessive protection; a globally representative international development agency in place of the World Bank, to manage certain modest development projects, minimise debt and assist countries to devise SOS strategies. Aid to developing countries should generally be for small-scale sustainable projects through locally based 'green villages' models. Such a system could be managed collectively via the UN, be funded by a global pro rata levy and benefits should be contingent upon countries adopting all SOS principles, while otherwise remaining fully autonomous politically, socially and culturally.

In the near future global programmes should be established for topsoil restoration, Third World debt repayment, reaforestation, reduction of population growth and energy conservation. The Worldwatch Institute has costed such programmes at US$729 billion by 2000 (MacNeill, 1990:120-1) which I reckon at less than 2.5 per cent of world income for the decade and less than one year's military expenditure. Even the US$1 trillion needed to retire all Third World debt and the several US$ trillion possibly required to alleviate global warming trends are substantially less than the total GDP of all OECD countries for one year (US$14 trillion). To fund such programmes a UN-administered international levy should be struck on all nations with per capita incomes of more than about US$10,000 per annum. Australia must continue its active role in international environmental forums and agreements, including the forthcoming UN convention on biodiversity and the much-disputed Toronto GHG targets. We must defy the growing band of greenhouse cynics and their suggestion that we wait to see if other countries adopt the Toronto targets (eg. Stone in *AFR*, 1 August 1991). The time has come to set a global moral example and be dinkum about saving our planet.

☐ MACRO-ECONOMIC STABILISATION

At the time of writing Australia is in recession with unemployment at about ten per cent and heading for a post-Depression record. At such times people are, understandably, inclined to lose some concern about the environment in a quest for jobs. ACTU president, Martin Ferguson, has recently said that the 'green lobby' has too much influence, that the ESD process will block certain development plans and has called for 'fast tracking' of large employment-generating projects (*Age*, 16 September 1991). This sort of view should, I believe, be avoided because it is based on the mistaken assumptions that environmentally-sound policies preclude employment growth, and that large resource projects create substantial numbers of jobs. The environment is no less in need of protection during recession than at any other time. However, the environmental movement has often been remiss in not making clear how jobs can be created while still protecting the environment, and in failing to adequately rebut the notion that accelerated growth is required to combat unemployment.

I argue that full employment can be maintained in an ecologically and socially sustainable manner through appropriate policy-making systems at the micro- and macro-economic levels. Micro-level policies would involve 'green restructuring' and continuing generation of the types of jobs discussed above, supplemented by special community-based job-creation schemes during a recession (eg. home insulation teams, tree planting programmes and so on). For the latter purpose pre-planned and costed 'shelf-projects' should be kept on hand. This concept was devised in Sweden and is now successfully used in a number of European countries, despite the criticisms of right-wing

109

detractors.[75] Such employment schemes, particularly where they are in labour intensive industries or services, could create substantially more jobs than large-scale capital intensive resource projects. However, micro-level programmes are not sufficient on their own to maintain full employment because market-based economies are characterised by five- to seven-year business cycles and periodic recessions. To counter this a comprehensive macro-economic policy system is required, although this concept is hotly contested by neo-classical economists and the New Right.

Western economies have experienced three major recessions in the past fifteen years, each cycle seeing a ratchetting of unemployment rates to a progressively higher plateau, the OECD average for the 1980s being 7.3 per cent and reaching 15-20 per cent in some countries. This has not, of course, prevented many Western governments from proffering economic advice to former CPS countries. Prescriptions for chronic macro instability have long been divided between two warring schools of thought — Keynesian interventionism and neo-classical laissez faire. The former school sees macro instability originating on the demand side when aggregate demand sticks at a level insufficient to employ everyone. Its recommended solution is that governments bolster demand by budgetary expansion, tax cuts and so forth. The latter school sees instability originating on the demand side with monetary disequilibrium, or on the supply side with disequilibrium in markets, primarily the labour market. The stock prescriptions are monetary control and competitive markets. Keynesian policies worked well for two decades, but by the 1970s they could not readily control inflation while simultaneously targetting production levels and unemployment rates. Governments have, therefore, gradually shifted favour to neo-classical approaches, even though the strict 'monetarist' version was generally abandoned during the 1981-2 recession.

An Australian variant of neo-classical economics and New Right philosophy, often referred to as 'economic rationalism', advocates de-regulation of almost everything, extensive privat-isation, slashing of public expenditure, micro-economic reform of inefficient markets, free international trade in goods and services and market-based environmental policies, with a modicum of intervention conceded in limited instances (IC, 1990:Ch.3). This school sees macro policy-making as largely 'neutral' or 'impotent'. There is a widespread view, with which I concur, that at present 'economic rationalists' monopolise policy advice in Australia to the virtual exclusion of all alternatives, and that the policies of both the federal government and opposition reflect this.[76] However, there is growing dissatisfaction with this policy-making tunnel vision, one bizarre result being that former icons of the Right, such as former Liberal Prime Minister, Malcolm Fraser (eg. *Sunday Age,* 1 September 1991), and B. A. Santamaria (eg. *Weekend Australian,* 28 April 1990), have expressed critical opinions about current macro policies which are to the left of the Labor Government!

I do not believe that the policies of the 'economic rationalists' are, in the main, ecologically, economically or socially sustainable, because their market-based environmental policies are inadequate; their free trade policies could exacerbate our structural dependence; their macro-economic policies have led to the current recession (through weakening fiscal measures and relying unduly on interest rate adjustments); and their general economic and social policies are adversely affecting social equity. It is important to understand that the 'economic rationalist' version of neo-classical theory is just one school of economic thought among a number available, including several revivified post-Keynesian streams. These alternative schools generally reject the concept of 'policy impotence', favouring some degree of macro intervention, micro regulation, exchange rate management and incomes policy. They have assembled a bevy of evidence that economies still operate in a Keynesian way and have designed new, modified Keynesian policy systems. Even some business groups are now advocating financial re-regulation and more active government policies.[77]

Perhaps the most sophisticated alternative macro model is that of the Cambridge-based 'New Keynesian' school led by Keynesian elder statesman and Nobel laureate, James Meade.[78] This model targets wealth and money GDP (its one item of agreement with monetarism) to control inflation, it targets wage growth to control employment levels and targets the exchange rate (via a flexible 'target zone') for external stability. The model allows plenty of scope for higher savings, capital spending (say on infrastructure and other capital works) and for a tax-funded expansion of the public sector. I suggest that, for environmental purposes, additional funds could be raised through pollution taxes, clean-up charges, fines, special purpose levies, resource rent taxes (at present gold mining is entirely untaxed), more realistic charges for renewable resources (eg. forests and water for irrigation) and more effective suppression of tax avoidance. We could also gradually, as required, raise our general tax ratio from its present depleted level of 30.8 per cent of GDP (almost the lowest in the OECD) to around the current OECD average of 38.4 per cent.[79]

A major weakness of the New Keynesian model is that it relies heavily on controlling wage costs through a rather vaguely defined concept of 'wage reforms'. In the Australian context I have suggested elsewhere (Dunkley, 1990) that cost-control could be achieved through a re-centralised, wage-price regulation system which I call a 'social contract-based incomes policy' (SCIP). Macro-economic stabilisation systems of this sort need not rely on environment-threatening growth just to generate jobs, because they would have various ways to influence the employment level. Such alternative strategies are worthy of more serious consideration than they are receiving in Australia today.

□ SCIENCE AND TECHNOLOGY

Many people believe, and I concur, that we are living in an age of technocracy and scientism whose mechanistic world view precludes other visions of reality. Insofar as science underlies the process of generating technical expertise it warrants adequate funding, although SOS principles would suggest a shift of research emphasis from sectors such as defence, 'Star Wars', nuclear weapons and power, high risk biotechnology or consumerism to fields such as biology, ecology, botany, agronomy, chemistry, medicine, 'soft' technologies, organic agriculture and the social sciences. Science, appropriately applied, can enhance our knowledge of Nature, discover how to divert itinerant comets from collision with the Earth and ensure the preservation of life on our planet.

However, insofar as science is also an instrument for policy-making in the way its information is used, and is a mechanism for value-formation in the way its epistemological prescriptions are promoted, it should be democratically controlled. Science should be a means, not an end. The process of translating scientific knowledge into technical innovation should also be democratically controlled through careful technology assessment, through monitoring by broadly representative governmental bodies in the green planning process and through the broadening of education systems to encompass human values, culture, tradition and critiques of the consequences of technology. Selection of technologies is done by people in institutional settings, not by immutable forces as scientism and linear technological determinism hold. The selection process must, therefore, be socially responsible, avoiding selections based on narrow profit-induced or greed-driven decisions. We are now entering an unprecedented epoch in which the ecological, social and cultural impacts of many technologies are potentially devastating. Thus, cost-benefit analysis of each technology must be more thorough than in the past, and we should stand ready to collectively eschew damaging products or technologies.

☐ SOCIAL JUSTICE AND EQUITY

It is a paradox of our times that just as CPS systems are collapsing and a US president designs to declare communism dead, many of the Western countries which boast of their superior stability are experiencing serious recession and social decay. Recently, while George Bush has been posturing around the world, the US Congress and other authorities have reported: — a falling GNP; declining real incomes for the lower classes; an underlcass of 50 million people who are racked with drugs, crime and other social crises; 90 million citizens have little or no health insurance; serious declines in educational aptitude scores; and a survey which found that 60 per cent of US high school children think the Ukraine is a sex organ (Walker in *GW*, 6 September 1991). Australia shares with the USA, a nation we seem determined to imitate, some of this social decay and the equal highest levels of child poverty in the OECD (Davis in SJC, 1991:224).

Throughout the Western world there has been a growing backlash, since about 1980, against the earlier rapid growth of the welfare state, the impetus for this coming from various sources such as conservative governments, New Right idealogues, taxpayers, cost-sensitive business leaders, 'economic rationalist' bureaucracies and so forth. Accusations against welfare and 'big government' are that they allegedly reduce work incentives, require burdensome taxes at 'disincentive' levels, induce tax avoidance, detract from productivity, reduce external competitiveness, create a class of people who are chronically dependent on welfare and so on. There are snippets of evidence for such claims, but no firm proof for any of them, including the persuasive but problematic notion of 'disincentives'. Inter-country studies reveal no clear correlation between public expenditure levels and economic performance (SJC, 1991; Dunkley, 1990). The New Right assault on welfare and redistrubtion is more ideological than empirical, and its success is due more to political influence than to valid social analysis.

The results of this backlash have been some useful expenditure reviews, some fat trimming and a few efficiencies, but also many social costs. In most Western countries social expenditures, infrastructure investment, government services, public housing and redistributive programmes have gradually been reduced, with the apparently direct result that poverty, inequality, social disorder and urban decay are demonstrably increasing. Such social problems have proved very sensitive to expenditure cuts and have often followed quickly thereupon.[80] In Australia the richest five per cent of people own half or more of the wealth, while all indicators of poverty and inequality are deteriorating. Government policies such as tax rate levelling, taxation anomolies which enable the rich to pay minimal tax[81], asset privatisation, expenditure cutting and pro-business policies (supposedly for developmental purposes) are rapidly exacerbating the situation (see Connell in SJC, 1991).

It is disappointing, to say the least, that this has happened under Labour governments here and elsewhere, but it will become even worse under conservative governments which are even more committed to the mechanisms that generate inequities. Historical experience suggests that distributional inequities are inherent in the very structure of market-based capitalism (see Winter in Le Grand and Estrin, 1989). Rising levels of social injustice and inequity do not augur well for the environment either, because many people will focus their concerns on economic survival and governments will resist additional claims on resources. In the short-term, social equity measures could only be funded, along with the projects urgently required for environmental improvement, by a government which is willing to raise the tax base from its current unrealistically low level. Virtually all areas of government responsibility would need bolstering from the additional revenue, and a progressive income tax scale should be restored to help reverse growing inequalities. This need not mean a restoration of old bureaucratic welfare systems, for decentralised, more participatory schemes linked to employment and other social programmes are possible. Some user cost systems might be retained, such as the 'higher education contribution scheme' (HECS), and more use should be made of means tests for certain welfare benefits. There could be some experimentation with market-based, efficiency-directed concepts such as 'vouchers', or socialist versions thereof, but on a limited scale because these are likely to have various inequities and anomolies (see Le Grand in Le Grand and Estrin, 1989).

In the medium-term certain new concepts can be experimented with, such as: — guaranteed minimum income systems; negative income taxes; a national superannuation scheme (see Mathews, 1989:116ff); taxation based on expenditure rather than income; improved versions of the wealth and inheritance taxes which many countries already have; low income savings schemes; new forms of public sector low cost housing and expanded housing co-op schemes (as in The Netherlands); and profit-funded community-based investment schemes (as in Sweden — see Mathews, 1989).

However, the experience of all welfare states to date, including social democratic versions, is that redistribution has been limited, poverty and injustice have persisted, bureaucratism has arisen and benefits have been reversed by unsympathetic governments. This is not because the principle of distributive justice is wrong, as the New Right infers, for the best results have been achieved in the best resourced welfare states, but because the most fundamental causes of social inequity have not been addressed. There are two categories of causes which should not be confused. The first involves differences in abilities, skills, initiative, education or luck, but these are the lesser cause, not the prime factor as the New Right seems to think. Such factors are partly natural, partly social and can be controlled through measures of the sort mentioned in the previous paragraph, although not all differences could or should be eliminated.

The second, more fundamental, category of causes of social inequity under capitalism includes: — rights to unlimited private property; unequal benefits from capital accumulation and technological change; rights to the proceeds of speculation and capital gains; inheritance; monopolistic practices; the extension of economic power to social domains (eg. media control) and to political influence, whether formally or corruptly. These can only be rectified in the long-term by extensive institutional reform, either by political revolution or by value changes conducive to reform. At present most trends, particularly the privatisation of public assets, are in the reverse direction. Feasible alternative social models have been proposed (eg. Robertson, 1989; Ekins, 1986), but implementing these would take time and some path-breaking value changes.

Perhaps the most promising alternative is the concept, with many possible variants, called 'market socialism', which seeks to use the market where financial efficiency is required and to invoke planning or redistribution systems where reallocation and administered equity are required. The centrepiece of market-socialism is a non-capitalist enterprise model, of which many versions have been proposed, including a share economy (Weitzman), labour-capital partnerships (Meade), socially-owned firms with umbrella entrepreneurial holding companies (Estrin) and a variety of co-operative models, some of which already exist (see Le Grand and Estrin, 1989). All of these have certain theoretical problems, but a likely long-term outcome is a co-existence of models ranging from a few large public enterprises, small- and medium-sized private firms, and various types of co-operatives, to networks of co-ops, communes, partnerships and individual traders. There is no need for a single enterprise model. In this system there would be room for some foreign investment but mostly via an equal partnership with local firms and under strict SOS guidelines. This would gradually moderate the global influence of TNCs with its associated economic and cultural dependence.

I propose that 'green-red' models should be of a market socialist type, with a mixed-enterprise system and most transactions being conducted through the market, though with requisite amounts of indicative green planning, green restructuring and macro stabilisation. Such a model would ensure social justice and equity by minimising large monopolistic private ownership within the enterprise mix; by using a range of community-based welfare measures (see above); by democratising all political, economic and social processes (see Mathews, 1989); and by providing women or other disadvantaged groups with enterprise options and general employment opportunities. The model would protect the environment by placing SOS principles at the centre of policy-making and setting appropriate systemic goals; by maintaining rigorous environmental policies; by de-emphasising growth; and by matching enterprise types to environmental tasks (eg. government contracts to green co-ops for environmental clean-ups, tree planting contracts to communal groups, etc.). Few greens have advanced any all-embracing alternative models, but the visions of those who have (eg. Brown, 1981) seem compatible with the above proposals.

The sorts of models discussed above are only theoretical at present, but elements of them have been used in practice by various countries with varying degrees of success. Many aspects of the Swedish model have influenced left-of-centre reformers for many years, along with regular prophecies of its downfall by the Right. Current recessionary problems and the September 1991 defeat of the Social Democratic Government have sparked yet more ill-informed prognoses of doom (eg. Clark in *AFR*, 16 September 1991). In fact, most aspects of the Swedish model are still intact, Sweden is the most egalitarian society in the West, unemployment remains minimal, social problems are limited and the OECD has forecast reasonable economic recovery for 1992.[82] The most influential and promising elements of the Swedish model are its welfare, social, training, redistributive, capital sharing, labour market and environmental programmes, although its wealth redistribution has been limited.

The Swedish case suggests that despite the ubiquity of capitalism and the frequent failure of social experimentation, alternative models could successfully sprout in more conducive political soil (see Elster in Paul, 1990). The rise of greener attitudes might provide such soil because a lower growth, soft technology, smaller-scale, domestically-focussed society based on organic agriculture would present far fewer opportunities for large scale capital accumulation or monopolistic practices than does our present-day materialistic society with its obsession for growth and competitiveness.

□ CULTURE AND VALUES

A crucial ingredient in the New Right's philosophy, and in its successful assault upon policy-making throughout the world, is its central assumption that human nature is egotistical, acquisitive, competitive, rationalistically optimising and that such traits are largely immutable. This image is eminently suited to the corporate interests which dominate capitalist societies, or which are in a position to socially construct and reinforce such images. The evidence suggests that these characteristics are but one pole of a spectrum of social norms, which are at least partly socially shaped and which can change over time. I have also suggested that ecological and social sustainability will require a shift away from this pole towards more co-operative, altruistic and ecologically conscious values, among other requisite changes.

Many theorists, including Marx and Keynes, have averred that we must maintain acquisitiveness and material incentives until such time as consumer satiation induces in people a more qualitative set of values. But there are three critical flaws in this notion. First, value change may be cyclical or irregular rather than linear and income-related, there being an apparent resurgence of materialism at present, for instance. Second, if this transition is very slow our ecosystems might not last long enough. Third, value changes may lead rather than follow economic trends. The processes involved are complex, but I argue that some autonomous value changes are possible, may be cumulative and can be catalysed by the individual or collective actions of 'change agents'.

Some of the directions I propose for value changes have been indicated earlier in the book, but I emphasise the following shifts:

- from competitiveness to co-operativeness;
- from egotism to altriusm;
- from anthropocentrism to ecocentrism;
- from struggle against Nature to harmony with Nature;
- from individualism to social consciousness (without excluding the possibility of personal fulfilment);

- from male dominance to equal participation of women's perspectives (what some call 'feminisation', though not all feminists see it this way);
- from acquisitiveness to simplicity, or what has been called 'conspicuous frugality' (Brown, 1981:356ff);
- from consumerism to a concern primarily with basic needs;
- more broadly, we require a re-definition of 'living standards' so as to break the nexus between income and incentives, and to counteract our obsession with productivity and economic growth.

Value shifts of this sort would undermine the assumptions upon which New Right policies are based, and would soon evolve new social goals. Concepts which dominate economic and political debates today, such as efficiency, competitiveness, economic rationality, markets or property rights (private for the Right, public for the Left), should be seen as means rather than ends, as they have tacitly become. The general goals of all societies should embody the ten sustainability principles which I proposed earlier.

Triggering a transition to such values will take time, and may involve the 'Catch 22' dilemma that a substantial shift in values might be required to initiate the institutional changes which would usher in the transition. As noted elsewhere in the book, there are signs of attitudinal change in opinion polls, but fewer such signs in the political arena, other than the advent of Green Parties. In many areas there has been a right-wing backlash, as with Australia's blue over green politics. Competitiveness expert, Michael Porter (1990:703-4 and 715), has berated Swedes for sacrificing competition and living standards to traditional egalitarian values, and Germans over their incipient taste for 'other dimensions of life'. But the predominant global trend is now toward wealth-seeking, consumerism and, at the urging of people like Porter, perpetual global rivalry or an international 'keeping up with the Suzukis'.

The barriers to transition are many, but I will note three. First, education is a vital channel for attitudinal development, but at present this institution is being pervaded at all levels by utilitarian, instrumental values oriented towards business. Second, print and electronic media are also crucial channels for conveying information or attitudes, but in most Western countries these are business-dominated, resulting in gross inequalities of power and influence. Australia is arguably the worst case in the West, with the main mass media being dominated by two billionaires (Rowe in SJC, 1991). Third, cultural globalisation and proliferation of US-dominated media is seriously depleting cultural diversity, purveying commercial, materialistic, aggressive values and greatly disadvantaging alternative value systems. In Australia's case such factors are, in my view, Americanising our identity, destroying our informal, ideosyncratic version of the English language, creating cultural (and other structural) dependency and making us a 'copying country' rather than a 'clever country' as we now import everything from political ideologies to the very language we speak.

Mechanisms which have been proposed for value change range from enhancement of 'green' education to revival of those religions which respect Nature (eg. Brown, 1981). Whilst I accept that all such institutions have a role to play, I believe that fundamental reconstruction is required in our cultural consciousness and information systems for the longer-term, though beginning as soon as governments can be talked into commencing the necessary reforms. Changes should include the following:

- massive reductions in concentration of media ownership;
- radio and television stations to be run by co-ops or community groups, rather than by business people, on a non-profit basis and geographically decentralised as much as possible;
- partial public funding of publications by small groups whose views would not otherwise be heard (as in Sweden — see Mathews, 1980:103-4 and 156ff);
- a 75 per cent local content requirement for television programming and a substantial quota for educational and cultural material;
- a strict upper limit on the volume of foreign television programming from any one country, so as to enhance diversity;
- minimal use of commercial broadcasting, the main funding coming from government, subscription or sponsorship;
- a long-term anti-consumerist programme by governments

which would: — gradually phase out most forms of commercial advertising; develop product information services rather than self-interested corporate promotion systems; shift taxation from income to wealth and expenditure; re-focus retailing from large shops and supermarkets to food co-ops and community markets (using minimal packaging);

- a 're-Australianisation' campaign to rescue traditional Koori and white Australian cultures from the pall of Americanisation now overcoming them.

These innovations should be part of a more general shift to a less materialistic culture which permits a range of philosophies and traditions to flourish. Science, economics and other such bastions of modernity have massively under-estimated the importance of culture, belief and spirituality to a social fabric, for many societies have totally collapsed when their culture was sufficiently undermined.[83] Societies require a balance between the material, the socio-cultural and a core of spirituality, the last-mentioned being broadly defined and non prescriptive of any particular religion or even religiosity *per se*. CPS systems may have collapsed through lack of such a balance rather than for primarily economic reasons. The main demands of the popular movements in former CPS countries have often been for religious and other freedoms, democracy, a cleaner environment and such like (see French in Brown, 1991). The West's problems are different but also lack this balance in a culturally and spiritually impoverished mass society. The reforms proposed in the previous paragraph could open the way for a massive change in values favourable to ecological and social sustainability, as well as for an exciting new cultural vibrance in Australian society.

□ TOWARDS THE 'GREEN-RED' MODEL

The exact shape of a 'green-red' model is difficult to anticipate and should not be too rigorously prescribed in order that many world-wide variations would be possible. Particular forms may develop more specific names, the terms 'eco-socialism' and the 'conserver society' being common in the literature already. The form I advocate could perhaps be referred to as 'green participatory socialism', though I have confined myself to the notion of a 'green-red' approach to sustainability. In Third World countries such a model may be an outgrowth of what I have earlier referred to as the 'green villages' approach. In industrial countries a 'green-red' model would require more drastic changes than in semi-traditional Third World societies, but there are embryonic models both in the literature (eg. Robertson, 1989) and in 'real world' alternative experiments. A 'green-red' model would differ greatly from the machine-chemical model, and to a lesser extent from the Pearce-WCED model, in being much less dependent on existing industries, technologies, high energy systems, chemical agriculture and large-scale organisation or on macro-economic growth and the global economic system.

In the short- to medium-term (the next decade or so) an Australian 'green-red' approach would: make SOS considerations central to all policy-planning; begin reducing RETP through resource and energy conservation programmes; legislate for a comprehensive system of environmental taxes and regulations; begin green restructuring, through a green plan directed at full employment, with emphasis on reducing environmentally damaging production, promoting exports, reducing imports and reversing our current structural dependence; introduce extensive waste minimisation schemes, involving both recycling and demand management measures; reduce immigration so as to achieve ZPG as soon as possible; raise expenditure on environmental restoration to perhaps around five per cent of GDP, with top priority being given to GHG reduction, CFC replacement, control of land degradation, waste minimisation and green restructuring; create separate national resource accounts and devise a qualitative measure of GDP; commence the requisite research for 'soft' technologies; begin implementing the social justice measures discussed above, with increased expenditures thereon if necessary; and commence the media and cultural changes discussed above.

In the longer-term, a 'green-red' model should seek to lay the foundations for a more ecologically and socially sustainable order in the twenty first century. The prime elements would include:
— all production, consumption, infrastructure and public service provision to be based on SOS principles and to be directed towards basic needs, social justice, social equity and inter-generational

equity; growth rates to level out and perhaps eventually decline to a more modest but comfortable level of per capita consumption; the economy to be based primarily on small-scale sustainable industries and organic agriculture; technologies to be predominantly 'soft' and of a 'post-Fordist', skill-enhancing type, centred on SOS principles and democratically monitored; an economic model based on a mix of market and planning, and on a range of enterprise types, with extensive employee participation in decision-making; de-centralisation of demographic structures; new urban concepts of land-sharing, facility-sharing and city farms; 'technology free zones' for people who wish to adopt simple, traditional lifestyles; declining reliance on international trade and TNC capital flows; much less cultural dependence; enhanced world cultural diversity; restoration of damaged environments; revival of appropriately sustainable traditions; and the fostering of non-material value systems. In general, governments must begin adjusting market demand and economic structures to environmental and cultural requirements, rather than the obverse as happens at present.

The political process by which a 'green-red' model would come into being cannot be anticipated precisely. In the West the process is unlikely to be an all-to-the-barricades revolution, even though the environmental movement already has its martyrs (see Day, 1989), for such an event has never occurred in a democratic, industrialised society. It may occur through newly emerging political systems in former CPS countries or certain Third World societies, but the aping of machine-chemical industrialism is rising ominously in these regions. The breakthrough is more likely to be an outcome of a dialectical process whereby changing social values and rising environmental awareness lead to 'green-red' government policies, and perhaps to coalitions of 'green' and 'red' political parties, this in turn leading to a further strengthening of ecological consciousness. Trade unions and a variety of non-government organisations (NGOs) can and should play a crucial grassroots role in this process. New social coalitions, such as between workers, farmers and environmentalists, may even, if politically unstable, periodically achieve critical legislative breakthroughs. Such a process may first occur in socially advanced Western societies like Sweden or The Netherlands, but there are also prospects in some Third World societies where simple, sustainable lifestyles maintain a presence. A rapid diffusion of the 'green villages' concept, which I discussed earlier, would greatly change the global development picture. Ultimately, I believe that a rising tide of 'green-red' values will become a natural successor to the welcome swell of democracy which is sweeping the world today.

7 CONCLUSION

In this book I have presented three sets of arguments. The first is that the machine-chemical form of industrialism, that which is incurably dependent upon capital, chemicals, energy, high consumption and the exploitation of Nature, is ecologically unsustainable, whether in a capitalist or socialist guise, because of its inherently harsh impact on the environment. Nor are the world's present political-economic systems, including Western capitalism, socially sustainable, as they are unable to deliver adequate social justice or equity, a deficiency which often forces people into ecologically damaging activities. The result is a world-wide, increasingly urgent, environmental crisis.

The second set of arguments is that orthodox solutions of the 'blue', or market oriented, variety cannot adequately deal with ecological unsustainability and do not really tackle social unsustainability. The much discussed Pearce-WCED model is an improvement upon standard 'blue' approaches, but this too is inadequate because its authors prescribe accelerated growth without any real assurance that their version of growth would be ecologically or socially sustainable. 'Red' schools of thought offer useful models for social sustainability and 'green' schools for ecological sustainability, but both are incomplete at present. The widely proffered view that we must seek yet more material wealth in order to divert some of it into patching up the environment is, in my view, a dangerous furphy. Material wealth is much more a cause of the environmental crisis than a potential cure. There are too many people in too many countries using too many resources, while too many people in other countries are forced by poverty into environmentally destructive pursuits.

My third set of arguments offers solutions which draw on 'green' approaches to ecological sustainability and 'red' approaches to social sustainability. In place of the misused concept of 'sustainable development' I argue that all human-made systems should seek to organise in an ecologically and socially sustainable way, irrespective of current economic growth rates or per capita income levels. I propose that all human activities be based on a four-tiered framework for the ecologically and socially sustainable organisation of systems (ECSSOS). Within this framework a number of institutional models could be used for social organisation, and I advocate a general 'green-red' model which draws on various 'light green', 'deep green' and 'red' traditions. Such a model would seek solutions to immediate environmental crises through more planned and decisive government action. It would also seek to construct long-term sustainability through more appropriate institutions, industries and technologies, through a more equitable distribution of wealth and power and through a shift to greater ecological consciousness and less materialistic values.

It is not possible to forecast the precise shape a society based on the 'green-red' model might take, but it would doubtless involve reductions in resource-energy throughput and new, simpler lifestyles, probably at per capita income and consumption levels (as currently measured) below those of today's machine-chemical economies. Such a society would not require a 'return to the caves' as some cynics jibe, nor 'much grimmer material standards' (Stone, *AFR*, 19 July 1990) nor 'condemning present and future citizens to needless poverty and hardship' (BCA, 1990:16). It would mean a transition to more basic and more assuredly sustainable living standards than prevail in the rich, 'over-developed' world at present, along with greater social equity and more spiritual satisfaction for all people. Nicholas Georgescu-Roegen, whom some consider an ultra pessimist, has suggested that humans could outlast the dinosaur's reign of 120 million years (in Daly and Umana, 1981:194), but this will not happen unless we abandon the machine-chemical economy and cease the current assault upon our planet. The longer we delay this transition, the fewer will be our options.

• NOTES

1. J. S. Mill, *Principles of Political Economy* (1848), Penguin, 1970:116.
2. William Morris, 'Art and Socialism' (1884) in *William Morris: Selected Writings*, ed. G. .H. Cole, Nonesuch, London, 1948:638-9.
3. For a choice selection of such accusations, see Kerin (1989); Haupt (*Age*, 15.7.89 and 17.3.90); Banard (*Age*, 25.7.90); Blainey (*Age*, 22.3.90); McCrann (*Herald*, 17.5.90); MacCallum (*Herald*, 10.4.90); Peter Walsh (*Herald*, 29.3.90); Desmond O'Connor (*AFR*, 23.8.90).
4. G. Sheridan, 'Green With Envy' *Weekend Australian*, 28-29 April 1990.
5. *Age*, 29 March 1990 and 1 August 1990. Also see C. Bean et al, *The Greening of Australian Politics: The 1990 Federal Election*, Longman, Melbourne, 1990.
6. Age Polls — *Age*, 6.11.89; 18.5.90; 15.2.90; 1.8.90; and ACF *Annual Report*, 1989-90.
7. *Age*, 18 April 1991:1 and 10; UK — *The Environmental Business Handbook*, Euromonitor, London, 1989:Table 4-3.
8. See Rowan Callick's review of Suzuki (1990a), Weekend Review, *AFR*, 30 March 1990. Also, Sheridan (Note 4) and Kerin (1989).
9. J. Passmore, *Man's Responsibility for Nature*, Duckworth, London, Second Edition 1980; Suzuki (1990a).
10. Literature on the debate is now vast. The classic 'pessimist' work is Meadows et al (1972) and the 'optimist' counterpart is Herman Kahn et al, *The Next 200 Years*, Morrow, New York, 1976. For recent 'pessimist' views Suzuki (1990a and b). For current 'optimist'

views see Max Singer, *Passage to a Human World*, Hudson·
Institute, 1987; Melvin A. Benarde, *Our Precious Habitat*, Wiley,
New York, 1989. For an Australian 'optimistic' perspective, Drake
and Nieuwenhuysen (1988).

11. BCA (1990); Wallis (1989); Australian Mining Industry Council,
Shrinking Australia, June 1990; Watson in *Mining Review*, May
1991.

12. The chief critics of Meadows et al were Herman Kahn et al (see
Note 10). The US *Global 2000 Report to the President* (1980)
up-dated Meadows et al in similar vein and was answered by J.
Simon and Herman Kahn (eds), *The Resourceful Earth*, Blackwell,
Oxford 1984. For a review of the issues, see Smith
(1979) and Ayers and Kneese (1989). 'Liberation' and perpetuity
— Solow (1974); Baumol, quoted in Daly, 1989:11-12; Thurow
(1981:111); BCA (1990:11); articles by Goeller, Barnett and others
in Smith (1979).

13. See estimates by Frosch and Gallopoulos in Scientific American
(1990:98).

14. Boum-Jong Choe, 'After the Metals Market Boom', *Finance and
Development*, June 1990:44-5. Bureau of Resource Economics,
Australian Resource Outlook 1987-2000, Research Report No. 1,
AGPS, Canberra, 1987.

15. *Economist*, 1990:25. Computers — Plunkett in *Business Review
Weekly*, 16 March 1990:8.

16. On this see Georgescu-Roegen in Smith (1979); Costanza in Daly
and Umana (1981); Daly (1989).

17. Consensus — WCED, 1990:218; shorter — UNEP (1987:Table 6-
2) and Frosch and Gallopoulos in Scientific American, 1990:98.
Oil optimists — Peter Odell and K. E. Rosing, *The Future of
Oil*, Kogan Page, London, Second Edition, 1983. Australia —
Department of Primary Industry and Energy, *A National Energy
Policy Paper*, AGPS, Canberra, 1988.

18. C. Flavin and A. B. Durning, *Building on Success*, Worldwatch
Paper 92, March 1988; Flavin and Lenssen in Brown (1991); L.
Schipper and A. Ketoff, 'Energy Efficiency — the Perils of a
Plateau' *Energy Policy*, December 1989; Goldemberg in Leggett
(1990:178) and Walsh in Leggett (1990:274). Energy-using bias —
Tietenberg (1989:486); Gever (1986:46ff). Trends derived from
OECD, *OECD in Figures*, various years.

19. *Economist*, 26 January 1991:27ff; International *Energy Agency
Review — Annual Report of Energy Policies and Progress*, 1989.

20. On these issues see H. and E. Odum, *Energy Basis for Man and
Nature*, McGraw-Hill, New York, Second Edition, 1981; *Scientific*

American, September 1971; Simmons (1989:239); Gever (1986); TWN (1990).

21. On USA — M. Reisner, *Cadillac Desert*, Penguin, New York, 1987; la Riviere in Scientific American (1990). On Victoria — information from Mr Jim Keary, Department of Conservation and Environment; *Age*, 18 June 1991. In general see WWF (1990:57ff).

22. Juhasz in *OECD Observer*, 160, October-November 1989; Milbrath (1989):183; Starr in *GW* 24 March 1991:19; la Riviere in *Scientific American* (1990). Dams — *Ecologist*, 14/5-6, 1984; E. Goldsmith and N. Hildyard, *The Social and Environmental Effects of Large Dams*, Wadebridge Ecological Centre, Camelford, 1984; F. Pearce in *New Scientist*, 25 January 1991; Shiva (1989); Flavin and Lenssen in Brown (1991:22).

23. Jacobson in Brown et al *State of the World 1989*, Norton, New York, 1989; P. Blaikie and H. Brookfield, *Land Degradation and Society*, Methuen, London, 1987; Walker and Young in *Land Economics*, February 1986; Krohe in *Ecologist*, 14/5-6, 1984:190; Crosser and Rosenberg in *Scientific American*, 1990; L. Brown and E. C. Wolf, *Soil Erosion: Quiet Crisis in the World Economy*, World Watch Paper 60, September 1984.

24. Beale and Fray (1990); Hawke (1989); Kerin — Speech to Fourth National Permaculture Conference, Albury, 6 April 1990.

25. Wilson (1988); Suzuki (1990a); Hawke (1989:18); Beale and Fray (1990); Hare et al (1990:28); WCED (1990:esp. Ch.5 and 6).

26. On views, trends, data, examples, anecdotes, etc. — see *OECD Observer*, 168, February-March 1991; OECD, *State of the Environment, 1985*, OECD, Paris, 1985; OECD, *Environmental Data Compendium* (Biennial); UNEP (1987); Commoner in Archibugi and Nijkamp (1989); Day (1989); Regenstein (1982); M. H. Brown, *The Toxic Cloud*, Harper and Row, New York, 1987; WCED (1990) and WWF (1990). On pollution in history see Simmons (1989). On China — V. Smil, *The Bad Earth*, Sharpe, Armonk, N.Y., 1984; Vermeer, *Ecologist*, 14/1, 1984 (reprinted in TWN, 1990:106ff); Li (1990).

27. In various publications and during a 1990 tour of Australia (see *Mining Review*, June 1990).

28. R. Bertell, *No Immediate Danger*, Women's Press, London, 1985; Day (1989:283ff); Keepin in Leggett (1990:313-4). Chernobyl — Dobbs in *GW*, 5 May 1991; French in Brown (1991:99). Diseases — Cribb in *Australian Magazine*, 24-25 August 1991.

29. Cancer and industry — S. Epstein, *The Politics of Cancer*, Sierra Club, San Francisco, 1979; *Ecologist*, 9/8-9, 1979 (reprinted in TWN, 1990:169ff); Earthworm, ABC Radio National, 30 January

1991; Regenstein (1982:Ch.7). Electromagnetic radiation — P. Brodeur, *Currents of Death*, Simon and Schuster, New York, 1989; *Economist,* 1 September 1990:79ff. Electronics — Forester (1987:71ff); WCED (1990:263); Bello and Rosenfeld (1990); D. Hayes, *Behind the Silicon Curtain*, South End, Boston, 1989.

30. *Acidification Today and Tomorrow*, Swedish Ministry of Agriculture, Stockholm, 1982; Pearce (1987); French (1990:22); WWF (1990:85ff).

31. Gosper — *Business Council Bulletin*, Jan-Feb 1991:18. McFarlane — in K. Coghill (ed), *Greenhouse: What's To Be Done?*, Pluto/ Fabian Society, Sydney, 1990. General policy issues — Leggett (1990); Coghill op cit; Australian and New Zealand Environment Council, *Towards a National Greenhouse Strategy for Australia*, AGPS, Canberra, 1990; Victorian Government, *Greenhouse: Meeting the Challenge*, Dept. of Conservation and Environment, Melbourne, October 1990. Refugees — J. R. Pollock for Australian Paper Manufacturers, Submission to Resource Assessment Commission, (No. FT/90/152A) 21 May 1990:Ch.F, p.6; I am indebted to Jenny Crawford for this reference.

32. Hawke (1989); Commonwealth (1990). Bureau of Agricultural and Resource Economics, *Age*, 28 January 1991.

33. P. M. Vitousek et al in *BioScience*, 36/6 June 1986:368ff; Ehrlich in Wilson (1989); J. Diamond in *Nature*, 328, 6 August 1987:479-80; Simmons (1989):esp.256; Daly (1989).

34. Tietenberg (1988):Ch.22; Dunkley (1989); WB (1990); A. Okun, *Equality and Efficiency*, Brookings, Washington, 1975.

35. W. A. Lewis, *Theory of Economic Growth* (1955) Allen and Unwin, London, 1970:424.

36. O. Giarini and H. Lauberge, *The Diminishing Returns of Technology*, Pergamon, Oxford, 1978; S. Ramo, *What's With Our Technological Society*, McGraw-Hill, New York, 1983; S. P. Schnaars, *Megamistakes*, Free Press, New York, 1989; Milbrath (1989:Ch.13).

37. Forester (1987); 'Total Factor Productivity', *Economic Outlook*, OECD, 42, December 1987:42.

38. C. Perrow, *Normal Accidents*, Basic Books, New York, 1984: UNEP (1987).

39. Cited by Ehrenfeld in Wilson (1988:213). In general see TWN (1990); Pereira and Seabrook (1990); P. Wheale and R. McNally (eds), *The Bio-Revolution*, Pluto, London, 1990.

40. Agarwal (1987); TWN (1990); Pereira and Seabrook (1990); E. C. Wolf *Beyond the Green Revolution*, Worldwatch Paper 73, October 1986.

41. Quoted by Milbrath (1989:257); Ehrlich — Science Show, ABC Radio, 24 February 1990.

42. J. L. Jacobson, *Planning the Global Family*, Worldwatch Paper 80, December 1987; WCED (1990:Ch.4).

43. D. Elgin, *Voluntary Simplicity*, Morrow, New York, 1981:128ff; H. Henderson, *Creating Alternative Futures*, Berkeley New York, 1978:395.

44. On these issues — R. Miles, *Awakening from the American Dream*, Marion Boyars, London, 1977; P. L. Wachtel, *The Poverty of Affluence*, New Society, Philadelphia, 1989; T. Scitovsky, *The Joyless Economy*, OUP, New York, 1976; D. Bell, *The Cultural Contradictions of Capitalism*, Basic Books, New York, 1976; J. Rifkin, *Time Wars*, Holt, New York, 1987; Durning in Brown (1991). Housework — S. Voumard, *Age*, 7 May 1991.

45. Post-Fordism — J. Mathews, *Tools of Change*, Pluto, Sydney, 1989; Mathews (1989); A. Gorz, *Critique of Economic Reason*, Verso, London, 1989. Post-Industrialism and 'economic sociology' critiques — F. Block, *Post-industrial Possibilities*, Uni. California Press, Berkeley, 1990; A. Etzioni, *The Moral Dimension*, Free Press, New York, 1988.

46. Mainstream — Thurow (1981:Ch.5). Socialist — Ota Sik, *For a Humane Economic Democracy*, Praeger, New York, 1985.

47. Max-Neef and others in Ekins (1986); Max-Neef et al, 'Human Scale Development' in *Development Dialogue*, 1989:1; WCED (1990:98-9). Also, Etzioni, op cit Note 45.

48. Alan Durning, *Action at the Grassroots*, Worldwatch Paper 88, January 1989; *Poverty and the Environment*, Worldwatch Paper 92, November 1989; B. Schneider, *The Barefoot Revolution*, Club of Rome, IT Publications, London, 1988; Pereira and Seabrook (1987); Agarwal (1987); Shiva (1989); A. Agarwal and S. Narain, *Towards Green Villages*, Centre for Science and Environment, New Delhi, 1989; I am grateful to the authors of this booklet for discussions on the 'green villages' model during their 1990 tour of Australia.

49. Treasury, *Economic Round-up*, 1989:19; F. G. Castles, *An ABC of R and D*, Discussion Paper No. 206, Centre of Economic Policy Research, ANU, Canberra, March 1989; other data from *OECD in Figures*, 1990.

50. All environmental economics textbooks outline the 'blue' approach, eg. Tietenberg (1988). 'Light blues' — Barbier (1989) and Pearce et al (1989). On valuation — D. Pearce and A. Markandya, *Environmental Policy Benefits: Monetary Valuation*, OECD, Paris, 1989; Pearce et al (1989); Tietenberg (1988).

Accounting — Y. J. Ahmad et al (eds), *Environmental Accounting for Sustainable Development*, World Bank, Washington, 1989.

51. Japan — Report of the NNW Measurement Committee, *Measuring Net National Welfare of Japan*, Economic Council of Japan, Tokyo, 1974; the original model was W. Nordhaus and J. Tobin, 'Is Growth Obsolete?' in *Economic Growth* NBER and Columbia Uni. Press, New York, 1972. US — Daly and Cobb (1989:482). UN review — D. Blades, 'Revision of the System of National Accounts', *OECD Economic Studies*, No. 12, Spring, 1989.

52. C. W. Clark in *Journal of Political Economy*, July-August 1973; Zarsky in ANU (1990:134). On property rights — IC (1990:Appendix 3).

53. Agarwal (1987); R. Wade, *Village Republics*, Cambridge UP, Cambridge, 1988; Perrings (1987:161); Roemer in Paul (1989).

54. The generalisations of the last three paragraphs are based on a wide literature, but in particular see: — General analysis — D. Pepper, *The Roots of Modern Environmentalism*, Croom Helm, London, 1984; Papadakis (1984). Precautionist 'red' — Enzerberger in *New Left Review*, 84, 1974; J. Weston (1986). Conservator 'red' — M. Bookchin, *The Modern Crisis*, Black Rose, Montreal, 1987; F. Dodds (ed), *Into the 21st Century*, Green Print, Basingstoke, 1988; E. F. Trainer, *Abandon Affluence*, Zed, London, 1985 and *Developed to Death*, Green Print, London, 1989; J. Seabrook, *The Race for Riches*, Green Print, Basingstoke, 1988; Robertson (1989); the journal *Capitalism, Nature and Socialism* (USA).

55. On 'light green' policy approaches see Brown (1981); Brown et al, *State of the World*, Norton, New York (annual); P. Ehrlich et al, *Ecoscience*, Freeman, San Francisco, Third Edition, 1977:Ch14; Daly (1977, 1980, 1989); Daly and Cobb (1989) — a somewhat 'deeper' green position. The 'ethical' approach — M. Sagoff, *The Economy of the Earth*, Cambridge UP, Cambridge, 1988.

56. The key Deep Ecology works are Naess (1989); B. Devall and G. Sessions, *Deep Ecology*, Peregrine Smith, Salt Lake City, 1985; B. Devall, *Simple in Means, Rich in Ends*, Peregrine Smith, Salt Lake City, 1988; *Ecologist*, 14/5-6, 1984 and 18/4-5, 1988; the journals *Environmental Ethics* (USA) and *The Trumpeter* (Canada).

57. Ecologist, *Blueprint for Survival*, Penguin, Harmondsworth, 1972; E. Goldsmith, *The Great U-Turn*, Green Books, Hartland, 1988; G. Dauncy, *After the Crash*, Green Print, Basingstoke, 1988; Ekins (1986); Robertson (1989).

58. Solow (1974); A. Nove, *The Economics of Feasible Socialism*, Allen

and Unwin, London, 1983; Paul et al (1989); Le Grand and Estrin (1989).

59. G. Dunkley, *The Prospect for Planning in Australia*, ANZAAS Paper, 1982 and *A National System of Environmental Planning for Australia*, Friends of the Earth, Melbourne, 1984 (Mimeo).

60. B. Mollison and D. Holgren, *Permaculture One*, Corgi, Melbourne, 1978 and successive volumes. M. Fukuoka, *The One Straw Revolution* (1978), Bantam, New York, 1985 and *The Road Back to Nature*, Japan Publications, Tokyo, 1987. In general, see TWN (1990); E. Wynen and S. Fritz, *Sustainable Agriculture: A Viable Alternative*, National Association for Sustainable Agriculture, Australia (NASAA), Sydney, 1987; and *Ecology and Farming*, journal of the International Federation of Organic Agriculture Movements (IFOAM). UK — *20% of Britain Organic by the Year 2000*, Soil Association, Bristol, 1990. USA — Langley et al, in *Agriculture, Ecosystems and Environment*, 10, 1983.

61. E. Dohlman in *OECD Observer* 162, February-March, 1990:32.

62. Green occupations — Brown (1981:266). Nett employment generation — OECD, *Employment and Environment*, Paris, 1978 and *Environmental Economics*, Paris, 1985:86ff; D. B. Brooks, *Zero Energy Growth for Canada*, McClelland and Stewart, Toronto, 1981; K. Ericson, *The Solar Jobs Book*, Brick House, Andover Mass., 1980; B. Hutton et al, *Jobs from Recyclying*, Friends of the Earth, Melbourne, 1983. On 'low cost' workplaces — Schumacher (1973).

63. Taiwan and South Korea — Bello and Rosenfeld (1990). Ireland — R. Allen and T. Jones, *Guests of the Nation*, Earthscan, London, 1990; Leonard, 1988:Ch.5.

64. See Pappas (1990); ESD (1991:98); 'Australia's Sustainable Future', *Business Council Bulletin*, August 1991.

65. Industries Assistance Commission, *Annual Report*, 1985-86:2-3.

66. See Banks et al in F. H. Gruen (ed.) *Australian Economic Policy*, Centre for Economic Policy Research, ANU, Canberra, 1991.

67. Treasury, *Economic Round-Up*, Summer 1990; *WB* (1990:Table 1).

68. Baldwin in *Economic Policy*, 9, October 1989; Neven in *Economic Policy*, 10, April 1990. Australia — Stoeckel cited in IC (1990:13).

69. *Economist*, 6 January 1990:17ff; P. R. Krugman, *Exchange-Rate Instability*, MIT, Cambridge Mass, 1989.

70. These and following import figures are based on ABS AICC data supplied by my colleague Jay Menon, though responsibility for analytical deficiencies is my own. For a broad and comparative break-down see *WB* (1990:Table 15).

71. On these concepts see: — Porter (1990); Pappas (1990); *Australian*

Manufacturing and Industry Development, ACTU, Melbourne, September 1990; *Networking and Industry Development*, Australian Manufacturing Council, Melbourne, April 1991; R. Kuttner, *Managed Trade and Economic Sovereignty*, Economic Policy Institute, Washington, 1989. For the contrary view, see IC (1990).

72. *Ecologist*, 20/6 1990; Shrybman in *Ecologist*, 20/1, 1990; R. Raghavan, *Recolonisation: GATT, the Uruguay Round with the Third World*, Third World Network, Penang, 1990. Tuna case — *Age*, 28 September 1991.

73. *General Agreement on Trade in Services*, Department of Foreign Affairs and Trade (undated draft); *Australian Traded Services and the Uruguay Round Negotiations*, Department of Foreign Affairs and Trade, Canberra, 13 June 1989. I am grateful to Ms. Meg McDonald of the Department of Foreign Affairs and Trade for information on these matters.

74. Quoted in D. Morris, 'Free Trade: The Great Destroyer', *Ecologist*, 20/5, 1990:190.

75. See Shirley Williams, *A Job to Live*, Penguin, 1985, esp. Ch.3.

76. See, for example, M. Pusey, *Economical Rationalism in Canberra*, CUP, Melbourne 1991; Dateline, SBS, 24 September 1991.

77. Darvall in *Age*, 9 February 1991; Millmow in *Economic Papers*, 8/4, December 1989; G. Hooke and R. Reilly (eds.), *Macroeconomic Policy*, Allen and Unwin, Sydney, 1991.

78. M. Weale et al, *Macroeconomic Policy*, Unwin Hyman, London, 1989 and references cited there.

79. From *OECD in Figures*, 1991:44-5.

80. On these issues see SJC (1991); Dunkley (1990); B. Hindess (ed.) *Reactions to the Right*, Routledge, London, 1990 and sources cited in each reference.

81. It has been claimed that Mr Kerry Packer, Australia's richest person, is able to arrange his affairs so that he personally pays less than ten per cent income tax (Four Corners, ABC, 16 September 1991).

82. See H. Milner, *Sweden: Social Democracy in Practice*, OUP, Oxford, 1989; OECD, *Economic Outlook*, 49, July 1991:102-3.

83. See T. G. Verhelst, *No Life Without Roots* (1987), Zed, London, 1990.

• BIBLIOGRAPHY

Argawal, A. et al (eds), 1987, *The Fight for Survival*, Centre for Science and Environment, New Delhi.

Archibugi, F. and P. Nijkamp (eds), 1989, *Economics and Ecology: Towards Sustainable Development*, Kluwer, Dordrecht.

ANU, 1990, *Moving Towards Global Sustainability: Policies and Implications for Australia*, Proceedings of National Workshop, 9-10 August, 1990 (CCE and CRES) Australian National University, November 1990.

Ayers, R. E. and A. Kneese, 1989, in Archibugi and Nijkamp (1989).

Barbier, E. B., 1989, *Economics, Natural-Resource Scarcity and Development: Conventional and Alternative Views*, Earthscan, London.

Beale, B. and P. Fray, 1990, *The Vanishing Continent*, Hodder and Stoughton, Sydney.

Bello, W. and R. Rosenfeld, 1990, *Dragons in Distress*, Food First, San Francisco.

Brown, L., 1981, *Building a Sustainable Society*, Norton, New York.

Brown, L., et al, 1991, *State of the World*, Norton/Worldwatch, New York.

Business Council of Australia (BCA), 1990, 'Achieving Sustainable Development', *Business Council Bulletin*, August.

Commonwealth, 1990, *Ecologically Sustainable Development*, AGPS, Canberra.

Crawford, J. et al, 1991, *Pulp, Paper and Perpetuity: Towards a Sustainable Future for the Australian Pulp and Paper Industry*, Masters of Environmental Science Dissertation, Monash University, Melbourne.

Daly, H., 1977, *The Steady State Economy*, San Francisco.

Daly, H. (ed), 1980, *Economies, Ecology and Environment*, Freeman, San Francisco.

Daly, H., 1989, 'Sustainable Development: From Concept and Theory Towards Operational Principles', *Ecological Economics*, 1:4.

Daly, H. and J. Cobb, 1989, *For the Common Good*, Beacon Press, Boston.

Daly, H. and A. F. Umana (eds), 1981, *Energy, Economy and the Environment*, American Association for the Advancement of Science, Washington DC.

Day, D., 1989, *The Eco Wars*, Key Porter, Toronto.

Drake, P. J. and J. P. Nieuwenhuysen, 1988, *Economic Growth for Australia*, CEDA, OUP, Melbourne.

Dunkley, G., 1989, 'The Public Sector — Crisis of Over- or Under-Spending', *Regional Journal of Social Issues*, Summer.

Dunkley, G., 1990, 'SCIPing the Accord', *Regional Journal of Social Issues*, May.

Economist, 1990, 'The Environment Survey', *The Economist*, 8 September.

Ekins, P. (ed), 1986, *The Living Economy*, Routledge and Kegan, Paul, London.

ESD, 1991, *Ecologically Sustainable Development Working Groups: Draft Report — Executive Summaries*, AGPS, Canberra, August.

French, H., 1990, *Clearing the Global Air*, Worldwatch Paper 94, January.

Forester, T., 1987, *High-Tech Society*, MIT, Cambridge, Mass.

Gever, J. et al, 1986, *Beyond Oil*, Ballinger, Cambridge, Mass.

Goodland, R. and G. Ledec, 1987, 'Neo-classical Economics and Principles of Sustainable Development', *Ecological Modelling*, 38.

Gordon, R. B. et al, 1987, *Towards a New Iron Age*, Harvard University Press, Cambridge, Mass.

Hare, W. et al, 1990, *Ecologically Sustainable Development*, Australian Conservation Foundation and others, Melbourne, August.

Hawke, R. J., 1989, *Our Country, Our Future*, AGPS, Canberra, July.

Industries Commission (IC), 1990, *Annual Report 1989-90*, AGPS, Canberra.

Kerin, J. 1989, *Speech to IBC Conference*, Mimeo, 1 November.

Leggett, J. (ed.), 1990, *Global Warming*, OUP, Oxford.

Le Grand, J. and S. Estrin (eds.), 1989, *Market Socialism*, OUP, Oxford.

Leonard, H. J. 1988, *Pollution and the Struggle for World Product*, CUP, Cambridge.

Li Ping, 1990, 'Environmental Protection in China', *Beijing Review*,

16-29 July.

MacNeill, J., 1990, 'Strategies for Sustainable Development', in Scientific American (1990).

Mathews, J., 1989, *The Age of Democracy*, OUP, Melbourne.

Meadows, D. et al, 1972, *The Limits to Growth*, Earth Island, London.

Milbrath, L., 1989, *Envisioning the Sustainable Society*, State University of New York, Albany.

Naess, A., 1989, *Ecology, Community and Lifestyle*, 1976 (Translated and adapted by D. Rothenberg), CUP, Cambridge.

OECD, 1989, *Economic Instruments for Environmental Protection*, OECD, Paris.

Papadakis, E., 1984, *The Green Movement in West Germany*, Croom Helm, London.

Pappas et al, 1990, *The Global Challenge*, Australian Manufacturing Council, Melbourne.

Paul, E. F. et al (eds.), 1989, *Socialism*, Blackwell, Oxford.

Pearce, F., 1987, *Acid Rain*, Penguin, Hammondsworth.

Pearce, D. et al, 1989, *Blueprint for a Green Economy*, Earthscan, London.

Pereira, W. and J. Seabrook, 1990, *Asking the Earth*, Earthscan, London.

Perrings, C., 1987, *Economics and Environment*, CUP, Cambridge.

Porter, M. E., 1990, *The Competitive Advantage of Nations*, Macmillan, London.

Regenstein, L., 1982, *American the Poisoned*, Acropolis, Washington.

Robertson, J., 1989, *Future Wealth*, Cassell, London.

Schumacher, E. F., 1973, *Small is Beautiful*, Blond and Briggs, London.

Scientific American, 1990, *Managing Planet Earth*, (Readings from September 1989 issue), Freeman, New York.

Shiva, V., 1989, *Staying Alive: Women, Ecology and Development*, Zed, London.

Simmons, I. G., 1989, *Changing the Face of the Earth*, Blackwell, Oxford.

Smith, V. K., 1979, *Scarcity and Growth Reconsidered*, John Hopkins, Baltimore.

Social Justice Collective (SJC), 1991, *Inequality in Australia*, Heinemann, Melbourne.

Solow, R., 1974, 'The Economics of Resources or the Resources of Economics', *American Economic Review*, May.

Suzuki, D., 1990a, *Inventing the Future*, Allen and Unwin, Sydney.

Suzuki, D., 1990b, 'Interview', *Habitat*, 18/3, June.

Tawney, R. H., 1921, *The Acquisitive Society*, Fontana, London, 1961.

Third World Network (TWN), 1990. *Return to the Good Earth*, TWN, Penang.

Thurow, L., 1981, *The Zero-Sum Society*, Penguin, New York.

Tietenberg, T., 1988, *Environmental and Natural Resource Economics*, Scott Foresman, Glenview III, Second Edition.

United Nations Environment Programme (UNEP), 1987, *Environmental Data Report*, Blackwell, Oxford.

Wallis, S., 1989, 'The Environment Debate', *Business Council Bulletin*, November.

Weston, J., 1986, *Red and Green*, Pluto, London.

Wilson, E. O. (ed.), 1988, *Biodiversity*, National Academy Press, Washington DC.

World Bank (WB), *World Development Report*, OUP, New York, annual.

World Commission on Environment and Development (WCED), 1990, *Our Common Future*, OUP, Melbourne, Australian Edition.

World Wide Fund for Nature (WWF), 1990, *Atlas of the Environment*, (G. Lean et al, eds), Arrow, London.

Australian Fabian Society:

The Fabian Society was founded in 1884 by Edward Pease,
Frank Podmore and Hubert Bland, joined by Bernard Shaw and
Sidney Webb. In Australia, the first Fabian group was formed in 1891;
the now Australian Fabian Society is a national organisation.

The Fabian tradition is one of achieving social progress through
research and education. The Society has no policy beyond that
implied in a general commitment to democratic socialism, and
issues its publications as the opinions of their authors, not of the
organisation. The publishing program is designed to promote
informed discussion on issues to further the goals of democratic
socialism.

• Membership details are available from:
**The Secretary, AFS, GPO Box 2707X, Melbourne 3001,
Australia.**

Socialist Forum:

The Australian socialist movement is small, lacks adequate strategic
thinking and is largely confined to the margains of political life. In
order to contribute to the renewal of the socialist project Socialist
Forum was formed in 1984 to promote new ways, new patterns of
thinking and a democratic orientation.

Some of our members belong to the ALP; others do not. We
provide an opportunity to canvass political, social and cultural issues
in an uninhibited way, free from the limits of factional party politics.
The achievement of a democratic form of socialism requires far-
reaching reform.

We believe this depends upon the activity of Labor Governments
sustained by popular support.

• Membership details are available from:
The Secretary, SF, PO Box 1056, Carlton 3053, Australia.